RIGHT TO PLAY

COLOFON

All rights reserved by Lemniscaat LLC • New York 2011 | © TEXT: Jesse Goossens 2005 | © TRANSLATION: John Tilleard 2005 | © DESIGN AND LAY-OUT: Marc Suvaal

Library of Congress Cataloging-in-Publication Data is available | ISBN 13: 978-1-935954-10-1 (Paperback) | Printing and binding: Worzalla, Stevens Point, WI

The English edition of this book has been made possible with financial support from NCDO, Amsterdam

RIGHT TO PLAY

EVERY CHILD HAS THE RIGHT TO PLAY

JESSE GOOSSENS - LEMNISCAAT

CONTENTS

FOREWORD

Every child has the right to play.

It seems so obvious; yet there are more than seven hundred million children who have never known what play means. That is about a quarter of all the world's children!

Johann Olav Koss, triple world skating champion and winner of four Olympic gold medals wants to make it possible that everyone, everywhere, will have the opportunity to play. 'Everyone' includes those children who, through war, natural disasters, violence or famine, have lost everything. It is for this cause that he has given up his career as a top class athlete, to take off again in a new direction. He founded the organisation, *Right To Play*.

This book tells the story of *Right To Play*.

I am taking you with me on a journey of adventure around the world. A visit, by reading, through the schools in Rwanda, refugee camps in Palestine, the slums of Mali and the United Nations Headquarters in New York. You will meet child soldiers who have returned from war, children who have to survive on the streets of Africa, and boys with nothing but a rolled up T-shirt as a football because they have nothing else to use.

You shall meet athletes from all over the world who will

tell you why they enjoy their sport so much, as well as famous ambassadors from *Right To Play* who will let you hear their memories of their early days of playing games and of their sports. From all these people you will learn why with heart and soul they are such supporters of *Right To Play*.

You will of course discover how the world's children play and take part in sport. It is through sport that they learn to live and play together and to lead others. Then their health gets better and they grow stronger whilst, at the same time, they find respect for themselves and others, too. But, above all, a lust for life enters into their young lives.

The cover of this book shows the familiar *Right To Play* symbol: a red ball. Anyone seeing a ball thinks at once of sport and play. Written on the ball are the words *'Look after yourself. Look after one another.'* This symbol provides instant recognition of the aims of *Right To Play*: a world in which all help one another. And that is what the organisation aims to achieve through the means of sport and play.

How does all this work in practice? It is in fact quite straightforward.

The United Nations tells *Right To Play* which refugee camps and disaster areas have the most serious need for its assistance. *Right To Play* sends out volunteers to these countries. The volunteers seek out the cooperation of any existing local organisations and get to work training youngsters from the locality in the arts of coaching. They then teach these new coaches how to get great games going with only the most simple of available means. Additionally, they are taught how to include girls as well as boys in sport; how handicapped youngsters can join in and gain so much from games and play. Information about healthy feeding is included, as well as attention paid to hygiene, diseases such as malaria, HIV /AIDS and the dangers inherent in tobacco and alcohol.

These coaches waste no time in getting to work amongst the children. As a project shows every sign of successful development, the *Right To Play* volunteers are brought home whilst the youngsters carry on with their sporting and their play.

As this book clearly shows, this concept has great consequences: children gain in health and happiness. The coaches take on a new aim in their lives. The atmosphere in the villages and camps is improved, whilst in furtherance of the *Right To Play* concept, other activities are organised for, as an example, the youngsters' parents.

But I am going on more than I should about the state of play! You will find it better to get involved, and you will find that far more interesting. Read with pleasure, feast your eyes upon the pictures, and play the games with your friends.

Look after yourself. Look after one another!

Jesse

EVERY

RIGHT TO PLAY

JOHANN OLAV KOSS

CHILD HAS THE RIGHT TO PLAY

Some ten years ago millions were glued to their TV screens as, like an inexhaustible comet, a young man in a shiny red outfit sped along an ice rink. There was an explosion of jubilation as he swept over the finish line. He had achieved what appeared to have been the impossible, having collected three gold medals and broken three records at the Olympics in Norway.

Johann Olav Koss was twenty-five when he ascended the stage of honour at Lillehammer with three gold medals around his neck. Already three times world champion, he was indisputably the world's finest skater. Yet he did the completely unexpected: he stopped.

'When I became famous as a skater,' Johann says, 'I became an ambassador for Olympic Aid and Redd Barna (Save the Children), a Norwegian organisation raising funds to help children in developing countries. It was through Olympic Aid that I was invited to come to Eritrea. I visited a variety of their projects during my week-long stay.'

FOOD OR BALL

Johann Olav Koss, walking through the dusty streets of an Eritrean slum area, notices a couple of lads sitting on a low wall along the way.

Greeting the lads with a 'Selam,' he strikes up a chat with them. 'Do you play anything at all?' he asks.

'Of course!' says one. 'We like to play football, but we can only do that when he's around.' And he points to a boy across the way.

He walks over to the youngster they had pointed to. The boy is wearing cut off shorts and a long-sleeved T-shirt.

Another 'Selam,' and Johann asks, 'How is it your friends only play football when you are around? Are you that popular?'

The lad says nothing, but takes off his T-shirt – a long-sleeved T-shirt – and knots the sleeves so as envelop the rest of the garment into a ball. He moves along to his friends, and then their game of football begins.

Johann stays awhile to watch their play. He takes out a ball he has brought with him to Eritrea, and hands it over to the youngsters. 'This is for you,' he says. 'And I promise you that I shall be back with more. I have to get on with my Olympics training, but after that you will see me here again with more sports equipment.'

A few months later, Johann is once more in an aircraft bound for Eritrea. The cargo hold is packed with sports material collected by children in Norway. Johann looks through a newspaper. There is an article written below a thick headline, 'Johann Koss takes footballs to starving children.' Now he begins to doubt if it really is such a good idea. Are people in Eritrea really going to be waiting for sports gear when they don't even have enough to eat?

By the time the aircraft lands, Johann is very anxious about the whole proceedings. What will be happening? Yet, as the passenger door opens and he steps out into the African heat, he knows that his anxieties have been unnecessary. There are over one hundred thousand Eritreans waiting for him.

When all the sporting equipment is loaded into cars, the parade is ready to leave. Ahead of the two kilometre long convoy of vehicles is Johann on a bicycle. Norwegian and Eritrean flags are being waved along the whole route. Everyone is dancing and singing. It is one enormous party.

After the ride, Johann meets the president of Eritrea. The president shakes his hand and tells Johann how happy he is with the arrival of sports gear. 'The children of Norway,' he said, 'look upon us as human beings, not mere mouths waiting to be filled. Food is not the only thing we are short of; we need just as much to bring hopes and dreams to our children.' And that is what Johann has done.

RIGHT TO PLAY

'When I was eleven,' Johann says, 'I knew, for sure, three things I wanted to do in life. I wanted to be a world champion skater, to study medicine and to be of help to children. Skating was the best thing that ever happened to me. I just loved to be on the ice and I found it great to be able to race just as hard as the older children. The skating club I belonged to was really pleasant, and one could hang around there forever. I skated together with my brother. Our father was always encouraging us. He used to say, "It's more important to get a little better each time, than actually winning."
That could well be true because my brother and I of course wanted to be the best.' Johann grins and continues, 'In fact I still hold to that!'
He considers for a moment and then says, 'While I was skating I learned something very important. Athletes – even the most successful athletes, myself included – lose more than they win. Yet there's no harm in that, as we all know that failure is a part of the whole. What is more, to become very good we have to accept many mistakes. They teach us a lot, whilst simply to get on with it is the most important! One can change one's tactics or try out something different, but one should never give up.
'Both my father and mother are doctors,' he explains. 'Their door was always open to all in need of help. For my part, caring about others and looking after others has always been the natural thing to do. My parents took me with them to show me different parts of the world. They took me to Africa, to Egypt and later on to India. That is why I can say that we in Europe are so privileged.
In this respect I had a remarkable experience at the age of fourteen.'

ALL OR NOTHING

It is summer and Johann Olav Koss is camping with sixty nine other boys and girls. One morning they get together for a nature trail. They were to have no breakfast.

Divided into groups of ten, every child was given a coloured card. Johann is the only one of his group to receive a green card. All the others have red.

The nature trail is exciting and leads them to a house. There, all those with green cards, seven boys and girls, are set apart from the others. Johann is with them. They are to come into the house; those with red cards are to stay behind.

As Johann comes in, he can hardly believe his eyes. In the room he has entered stands a large table overflowing with a mass of goodies such as ices, chocolates, cakes and all one could imagine. Around the table are seven seats. Without a second's thought, Johann and his friends rush to the table.

RIGHT TO PLAY

the other. A boy beside Johann starts to throw up. He gets hold of a large cake carton, pukes into it, pushes the carton to one side and gets back to stuffing himself. Johann cannot believe what he is seeing but is unable to stop eating.

Then the expected happens: the sixty-three youngsters in the other half of the room storm in through the plastic curtain to run up to the table. Johann and the others at the table escape as fast as they can and out of the room for fear of falling under the feet of the other group.

'I founded Right To Play so the world should be a healthier, safer place for children,' Johann explains. 'I think that can happen through sport and play. Why? Take a few hundred boys, put them somewhere where there is nowhere else to go and nothing for them to do. What happens next? They start looking for trouble.
In refugee camps and internally displaced camps all over the world there are eleven million men and boys. They have nothing to strive for, no hope of a better life, and there is nothing for them to do. Then the problems start; violence and sexual abuse rear their ugly head, there is no schooling for the children and adults start neglecting themselves. Yet if you can give them something to do, such as taking part in sport and in play, some sense of meaning enters their lives.

By this time they have a raging hunger, so they attack all that wonderful food. They are eating with both hands and as fast as they can get it down.

But Johann notices that something is happening on the other side of the room. He can see a wall that is made of a great plastic curtain. He can hear the sixty-three youngsters who, with their red cards, have been let in behind that screen. Although he is unable to see the children, it is clear to him that they do not have the same range of good things as he sees on the table before him. This is now becoming apparent to all the children at Johann's table, each now trying to eat faster than

That is what we are doing in Right To Play, we return that power of courage and strength to young and old through sport and play.

To give one example: in Sierra Leone we are working with UNHCR to train our coaches in the basic skills of sport and play. Because football was the most popular sport, our local refugee coaches asked if they could get a more specialized football training. In partnership with the international football association, FIFA, we started a specialized football coach and referee training for refugees who had fled from Liberia. These youngsters are now coaching teams within the refugee camp. They became so confident in their abilities that they are keen to return to Liberia to coach at the national level. Women and girls are finding sporting activities and play just as important as the men and the boys. Participation in sport leads to increased self-confidence. They find new respect for themselves and for their bodies. Everyone is the better for it.'

A NEW LIFE

Johann Olav Koss is in Sierra Leone on a visit to a *Right To Play* project. Passing a training centre where girls are taught to sew, he comes across a girl of fifteen or so leaning against the wall. She looks thoroughly miserable.

'What's the matter?' Johann asks.

'I think I shall be going back,' the girl replies.

  'Back? Where to? Where have you come from?'

  'Back to the rebels,' says the girl.

The girl explains that she was a child soldier. During the war she was serving the rebels in the field, cooking for them and doing their washing. She became pregnant from one of the rebels and had a baby daughter. 'When peace came, I went back to my village,' the girl tells Johann, 'but the people in my village think it brings shame that I should have had a child by one of the rebels. And my parents do not accept my little daughter. No one is kind to me. There is nowhere I can go to. All right, here!' she says, pointing to the building behind her. 'I get sewing lessons, but what good does that do if there's no one who will talk to me? I really think I will leave.'

'Do not go back – please,' Johann begs her. 'If you promise to wait a while, we shall see what we can do to help you.'

Johann feels that there must be something that can be done. Together with members of *Right To Play* in Sierra Leone, he works out a plan. They will put the girls from the training centre on a course of coaching. Every day, for an hour or two, they are going to participate in some sport and take lessons in how they, themselves, can best play with children. So there will be something for them to look forward to.

RIGHT TO PLAY

After some months, Johann receives a letter. The sender is the girl that he had met in Sierra Leone. She writes to him with the news that her life has absolutely changed. She finds it wonderful to be taking part in the activities, and she is thoroughly enjoying what she is now doing. She makes friends and is finding herself a fully accepted member of the group. In between times, her parents have come to accept the new situation. Together with her daughter, she has been re-admitted to the family.

'With Right To Play we want to give children hope. We want to have them laughing again and give them back their dreams. And it does happen.
One of our international volunteers from Canada, Maggie McDonald, told me of a large sports festival in one of the camps. Thousands of children were there to take part, and by the end of the festival everyone was truly happy.
When the party was over, Maggie noticed a young lad on his way with a banana in his hand. The boy met up with a child who had nothing to eat. Breaking the banana in half, the boy shared it with the other, saying, "Look after yourself, look after one another."
That is just what it is all about.'

MA

FACTS OFFICIAL NAME Republique de Mali
MOTTO One People, one Goal, one Faith (Un peuple, un but, une foi)
AREA 1,240,000 km² POPULATION (2005) 12,291,529
CAPITAL Bamako CURRENCY Cefa (Communauté Financière Africaine
franc) LANGUAGE French, Bambara, numerous African languages
RELIGION 90% Muslim, 9% native religions, 1% Christian
LIFE EXPECTANCY (YEARS) 45 AVERAGE DAILY INCOME € 1,89

RIGHT TO PLAY

LI

It is 3:30 in the morning when I am startled from sleep by an announcement. It takes a while before I realise that I am in the plane that left Casablanca three and a half hours ago. 'Ladies and Gentlemen,' the announcement through the intercom begins, first in Arabic and then in French. 'We are starting our descent to Bamako. You are kindly requested to put your seats in the upright position and fasten your seatbelts.'
Around me the other passengers are waking up. Women are in brightly coloured, wide dresses with matching headgear of striking intricacy. The men are clad in the traditional long flowing boubou, sometimes worn over trousers, or wearing a western style three-piece suit. The sounds of cheerful chatter get louder and louder as the lights of Bamako come into focus through the cabin windows.
By popping, my ears are protesting against the aircraft's sharp descent. I can already see the runway, and the plane seems to be but a few metres off the ground when the engines suddenly open to a wild roar and all the passengers are pressed against their seats as the machine is once more powered into ascent.
The lights of Bamako begin to recede and finally disappear from sight.

What is going on? There is a deathly silence in the cabin. In the aisle, the little screens we watched during the flight to see how high, how far and how fast we were flying, are showing nothing more than a test image.
There is no sign of any of the flight attendants, and there is not a word from either pilot or purser. Twenty minutes go by, extremely slowly. The aircraft makes an occasional change of direction to the left or to the right. No one dares utter a word.
Suddenly a startling noise as of pandemonium; it is the landing gear being lowered. This vital action, it would seem, had been overlooked at the initial attempt to touch down. There could have been quite a belly flop!

Once more the aircraft begins its descent. The runway lights come close again. I can see the red earth next to the tarmac strip and feel a tremble through the plane as wheels meet the ground. A sigh of relief flows through the cabin; gradually conversations are continued as the machine taxies toward the arrival hall.
I am in Mali.

Drapeau

A favourite, traditional game in Mali is Drapeau ('F'laq').

The group of players is divided in two. A game leader holding a flag takes position in the middle of the field. It is of course the green, yellow and red flag of Mali.

The two groups stand, each in a long row, on opposite sides of the field. So there are now two opposing rows of players, with a game leader in the middle.

In both groups everyone is given a number, beginning with 1, the second takes 2 and so on.

The game can begin.

The game leader holds out the flag and calls a number. From both groups the player with that number runs to the middle as fast as he can to get the flag.

The first one to arrive at the flag grabs it and runs back with it to his group, there to 'plant' the flag. But at the moment that the one player has taken the flag, the other can chase him. Should the other succeed in touching the flag bearer before he can plant the flag, the flag bearer is out. Should the flag be planted, the winning group is awarded a point.

The players stand in line again; the game leader picks up the flag and gets the game under way as he calls another number.

In front of a high wall there is a board with the well-known red ball: *Prends soin de toi. Prends soin des autres* – Look after yourself. Look after one another. By the gate in the fence in the wall a Malian boy is sitting in a garden chair. He barely raises his head as I go through. He is the guard at the Right To Play office.

The office, where two of the three volunteers live, is a decrepit white bungalow with doors and windows barred against burglars. Inside, two fast spinning fans are driving away the desert heat.

On the low benches sit six Malian young men and one woman. They are having a meeting with the staff of Right To Play. They are coaches who have been involved in a measles campaign.

In Mali, Right To Play is working on a SportHealth programme. This involves not merely the organisation of sport and play programmes, but the cooperation of Right To Play with a variety of different organisations – Malian as well as international – to ensure an improvement in the country's health care.

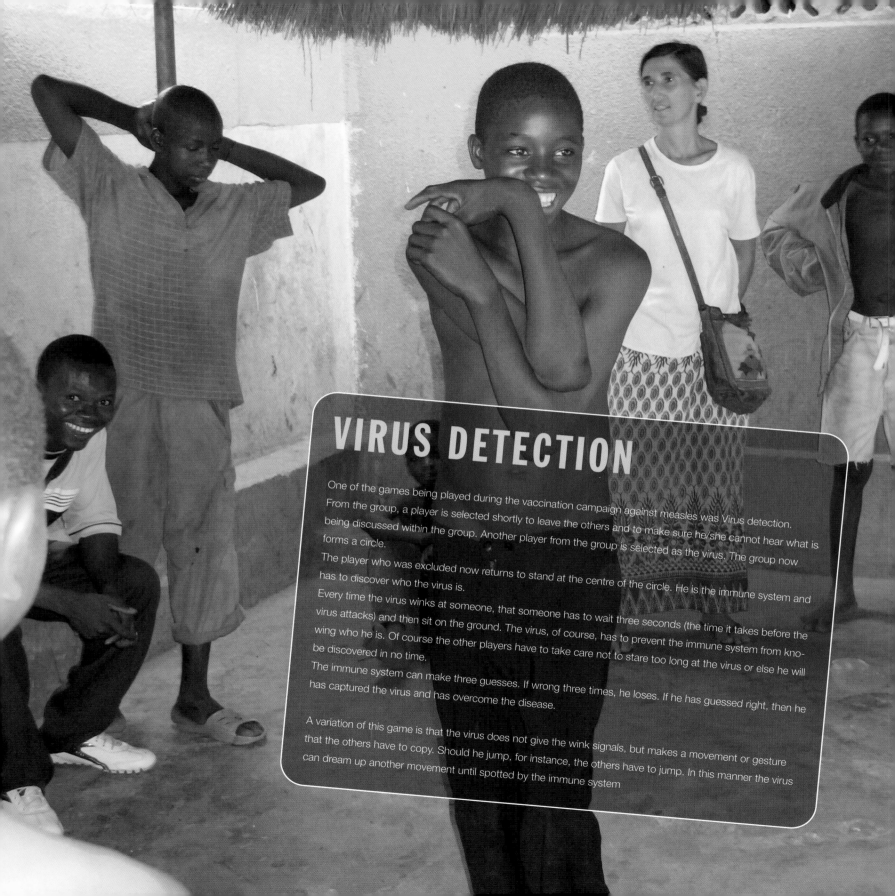

VIRUS DETECTION

One of the games being played during the vaccination campaign against measles was Virus detection. From the group, a player is selected shortly to leave the others and to make sure he/she cannot hear what is being discussed within the group. Another player from the group is selected as the virus. The group now forms a circle.

The player who was excluded now returns to stand at the centre of the circle. He is the immune system and has to discover who the virus is.

Every time the virus winks at someone, that someone has to wait three seconds (the time it takes before the virus attacks) and then sit on the ground. The virus, of course, has to prevent the immune system from knowing who he is. Of course the other players have to take care not to stare too long at the virus or else he will be discovered in no time.

The immune system can make three guesses. If wrong three times, he loses. If he has guessed right, then he has captured the virus and has overcome the disease.

A variation of this game is that the virus does not give the wink signals, but makes a movement or gesture that the others have to copy. Should he jump, for instance, the others have to jump. In this manner the virus can dream up another movement until spotted by the immune system

A PARTY FOR A VACCINATION

Kebe can see the big banner from the distance: 'Right To Play' it reads, in big red letters on a yellow background. The banner matches Kebe's T-shirt. On it is the red ball with the motto *Prends soin de toi. Prends soin des autres.*

In daily life Kebe is a medical student at the University of Bamako. But today he is what the coaches of *Right To Play* in Mali are called: *formatteur*. A month ago Kebe heard that the organisation *Right To Play* was looking for volunteers who would be trained to become *formatteur* and help with the big measles campaign that was being set up by the Mali government. He applied at once.

Kebe is well aware of the dangers from measles. During his studies he has learned that in the African countries south of the Sahara half a million children die of this disease each year. This is by no means necessary, as a single injection can save a

life. Yet whereas in Europe or America the school doctor or the family physician inoculates everyone without delay, Africa's children are far more difficult to reach. Many children do not attend school; most people have no regular doctor, whilst the dwellings and the villages are far apart.

Kebe can well imagine that few are prepared to walk a few kilometres for an inoculation. That is why he felt it was a good plan for *Right To Play* to organise sports festivals where the children would be able to play and to take part in sports. Undoubtedly many children would come and, with the sports and the games, they would also be enabled to learn much about measles and other diseases.

For two weeks Kebe underwent training in which he learned how to interact with the children and through what games he could teach them something. He saw how famous football players from Mali promoted the Play Day of *Right To Play*. He

heard too how more and more children from the neighbour-hood began to look forward to the coming festival.

A small piece of paper is lying on the ground. Kebe picks it up and smiles. It is one of the flyers that *Right To Play* has had printed. Against a bright blue background, there is Frederic Kanouté the Malian footballer, playing for Tottenham Hotspur. He is wearing a yellow *Right To Play* T-shirt and holds a red ball under his arm. 'I support the vaccination campaign against measles,' is the message in the text balloon above his head. Kebe has also seen advertisements with Seydou Keita, midfielder for RC Lens and with former coach Capi.

Kebe feels right on the ball. He will make sure that the children have so much fun today that the injection will be very swiftly forgotten. Walking up to the sports ground he can hard-ly believe his eyes. There are already more than two thousand children waiting for the sporting festival to begin. That will be quite something for his first day as *formatteur*. There is one thing for sure: the *Right To Play* campaign is working!

MOUSSA AND THE MARABOU

Moussa walks with his tomato can past the cars on the crossing. It is warm, although the morning is still young. The folks in the cars have opened their windows. Moussa is poking his can inside every car, as he calls for 'A little money for the marabou please…'

It is a little over a year since his father sent him to the marabou.

A marabou is a wise man, a religious leader as well as a sort of medicine man. In Mali nearly everyone is Muslim, but most Malians also believe in the ancient forces of nature. When there is a problem, a Malian goes to see the marabou. He gives advice when someone is going through a hard time, or he makes a *gris-gris*. A *gris-gris* is a small bag tied around the arm as protection against evil, against disease or against problems. In such a bag may be herbs, small pieces of rock or bone, pieces of cloth, notes with spells, hairs, nails, small dried insects – all manner of objects. For every problem and for every affliction another *gris-gris* is made.

Moussa used to live in a village, a hundred kilometres outside Bamako. There he grew up with his six brothers and sisters. Moussa was the oldest of the children and his father wanted him to become a good Muslim.

Because there was no school for the Islamic faith in the village, Moussa was apprenticed to the marabou, meaning that he was taught at one and lived there.

The marabou had a good forty students, but lacked the money to feed everyone. Yet this was no problem to the village. The marabou's apprentices went around the houses and would be given some food from every villager who had any left over. In this way everybody in the village helped the marabou and his students. Moussa liked it; he learned much and made friends among the other apprentices.

The time came when the marabou decided on a move to the city. A good number of the children went with him, and Moussa's father thought it a good idea that his son as well should go to Bamako. He had never had that kind of opportunity and felt Moussa could probably learn more there than in the village.

In Bamako everything changed. The marabous in the city didn't let the students ask for food, but for money, so they could buy the food themselves. Moussa's marabou as well thought that was a good idea. Just like the other marabous he collected tomato cans and cut off the tops. As everyone in Bamako knows, when a boy with such a tomato can comes to ask for money, he comes for the

marabou. There are many who give a few cefa every day to a marabou's child.

The marabou could see that there was money to be made this way, and not just for feeding his students, but for much more. So he wanted his boys to come home with more money every day. After a while he was demanding as much as three thousand cefa a day. Anyone failing to collect enough would be beaten.

After Moussa had been thrashed for the umpteenth time, he decided not to go back to the marabou. Since then he has been living on the street. He still begs with his can, but now to collect money so as to be able to feed himself. He knows that he has to be careful, because if a marabou gets to know that a boy is collecting for himself with a tomato can, he will be given a beating that would take time to forget.

Unsurprisingly, Moussa is startled when he hears his name. 'You're Moussa, aren't you?' asks a man in a colourful traditional *boubou*, on foot amongst the cars. Moussa is ready to run off, but the man says: 'Don't be afraid, Souliman gave me your name.'

Moussa hesitates. He remembers Souliman from his old village. He was also a child of the marabou and had come to the city. Souliman had run away from the

RIGHT TO PLAY

marabou a couple of months ago and has been seen now and then by Moussa on the street.

'I am Félix,' the man tells him. 'I want to help you. Do you know the relief centre in Quinzambougou?'

Moussa nods, but doesn't say anything.

'We are going to play there, later on,' Félix says. 'Just have some fun. Souliman will be there as well. If you get there in good time, you can join us when we eat together.'

Moussa is well aware of his empty stomach. But can he trust this man?

'It's up to you,' Félix tells him. 'I'm there every day, so you can also come at some other time.' He moves on through the traffic.

Moussa sees the colourful *boubou* vanish into a side street. He thinks for a moment and then walks slowly in the direction of the relief centre.

A high wall fences off the relief centre for the Quinzam-bougou district. The gate is wide open. In the play area in front of the centre some thirty boys between the ages of eight and fifteen are playing. Two groups are loudly supporting a game of table football. There is dancing to souk music from an old ghetto blaster. On a low wall two boys are bent over

a draughts board, whilst further along another is constructing a rifle from pieces of Lego. He raises his head at the blast of a whistle. A game leader is standing under a reed-built shelter. All the boys run over to him and form a circle around him.

When I walk about to take in the activities, I notice a can lying in a corner. The top has been removed, and the red-white print on the side is beginning to rust away.

I hear a man's voice, 'That's Moussa's can.' Turning around I see a man in a colourful boubou. He shakes my hand and introduces himself as Félix, the manager of the relief centre. 'It's Moussa's first day here. He is the boy over there in the middle.'

There under the shade is a group of boys playing a circle game. A boy with a wide grin on his face is standing in the middle, trying to guess who in the circle is giving secret signs to the other children.

'All the enfants de la rue, the street children who come here, have their own story,' Félix relates. 'There are boys like Moussa who ran away from their marabou, children who had nothing to eat at home, because their parents couldn't afford food, refugees who escaped from child dealers that tried to sell them as cheap labourers to countries like Ivory Coast, and children who were abused at home. We meet up

FISH HUNTER

The group of players is divided into two.

One group moves some distance from the other.

Out of earshot from the other, one group chooses a number. Then they form a circle – a fishnet – hand in hand, stretching out as far as they can to form a series of gates so that players in the other group are able to run under the outspread arms, into the circle. Those running in are the fish that have come into the fishing net and should now try to get out as quickly as they can.

As soon as the encircling players start counting, 'one, two, three, four…' that is when the others have to start running, diving into the circle and trying to get to the other side as quickly as possible. But at the moment that the players in the circle get to the number they had chosen, they drop their arms and bend their knees. The fishnet is closed. All the fish that are still in the net are out.

The game is repeated until all the fish are caught.

with them on the street,' Félix says, 'and we invite them to come to the centre.

One of our first actions here is to check on their state of health. We talk with them and then we try to find their family – everybody has family, even if there are no parents there will be an older brother, uncles or aunts or grandparents. When a boy is ready, we go home with him. There is always one of us who goes along to see if he has a good, safe shelter. But until that day we make sure he at least has enough pleasure in his life. From Monday to Thursday the boys get breakfast here. They can come to our centre for medical care and of course we have our game mornings – three or four times a week. The game leader you see there is trained by Right To Play. It is the games he plays with the boys that make them come back to the centre each time. Everyone can play soccer on the street, but the group games we do here give the boys so much fun they don't want to miss a single morning.'

A loud cheer from within the playing circle seems to affirm those words from Félix.

There is cheerfulness about the painted walls of the Centre d'écoute in Sikoro. Within, there is a scene of lively activity. About a hundred children are bent over board games and

cards. Some are playing draughts, some four-in-a-row, others at happy families, Risk and a variety of well-loved card games, whilst in one corner a girl is reading from a picture book to some younger children.

Because it is so warm in Mali, board and card games are very popular. You cannot play football and other games calling for a lot of running about at the hottest time of day. Right To Play makes sure that the packs they provide to the centres include a good mix of board games. Games made in the vicinity are preferred as their purchase helps local people to earn some money.

In the Centre d'écoute of Sikoro the older children make games themselves: boxes of bricks, draught-boards, shove-halfpenny boards, colourful game boards made from wood and elastic bands. These games are sold so that new materials can be bought. And of course the children play with the new stuff too.

When the worst of the heat is over, around five in the afternoon, a long line of children, accompanied by two game leaders, walk to the stretch of sand in front of the centre. The group is divided in two, and the game can begin.

I notice a small girl with a little boy on her back is staying at the side.

A LITTLE BROTHER ON YOUR BACK

'I don't mind if you go to the *Centre d'écoute*,' Aminata's mother tells her. 'But you will take Habib along with you.'

She pulls Aminata towards her and ties her one and a half year old brother in a blue baby sling on her back.

Habib is heavy, but Aminata is used to carrying him. She is already six and old enough to look after her little brother. While he is being carried uphill to the centre, Habib, with his big black eyes, takes in everything that is going on around him.

The centre is a very nice place to be. Today, there are guests from another country, and music is made for them. Aminata sits by the water hole, making sure Habib's little legs don't get stuck. She listens to the cheerful guitar music and sees how the musicians keep playing while they are dancing themselves into a frenzy. As the music stops, she walks over to a corner of the centre where a girl is reading from a book full of colourful pictures. Aminata likes coming to the *Centre d'écoute*. There are always other children to play with.

At the end of the afternoon all the children go outside to do round games. Aminata walks along with the group, but stays at the side. When she is standing still, Habib hangs heavily on her back. Every few minutes Aminata lifts him up over her narrow hips.

She would love to play along with the children who are enjoying Fish hunter in the big circle. But that she cannot do as it would be dangerous to run with her little brother on her back.

'Should I hold your little brother?' she hears someone asking in French. Aminata looks up. Next to her, one of the foreign guests is standing. It is a tall girl that has a whiter skin than Aminata has ever seen before. She has long blond curls and is wearing a little hat against the sun.

'Let's have him!' the girl says.

Aminata doesn't have to think twice about it. She quickly unties the sling and hands Habib over to the girl. She watches how the white girl takes her little brother on her arm. Habib seems to be perfectly happy with it all. Aminata's back begins to relax. It's a good feeling, and she sighs with relief.

She feels a little push from the white girl who says 'Go on! Go and play with the others. I'll look after your little brother.'

Aminata looks at the playing children. She would love to join in, but she really can't. Her mother told her to look after Habib, so she cannot leave him out of sight. She stays next to the white girl, so she can see that all is well. After a while her back is not quite so tired.

Aminata signs to the white girl that she wants her little brother back. A woman from the centre helps her to tie Habib up once again.

RIGHT TO PLAY

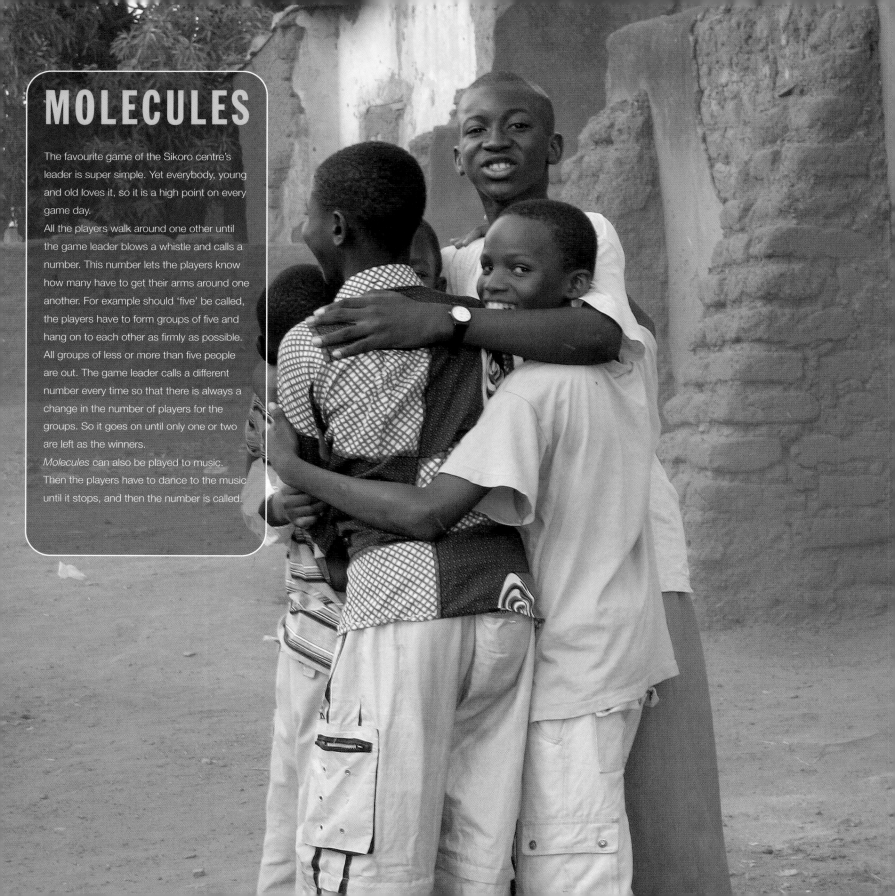

MOLECULES

The favourite game of the Sikoro centre's leader is super simple. Yet everybody, young and old loves it, so it is a high point on every game day.

All the players walk around one other until the game leader blows a whistle and calls a number. This number lets the players know how many have to get their arms around one another. For example should 'five' be called, the players have to form groups of five and hang on to each other as firmly as possible. All groups of less or more than five people are out. The game leader calls a different number every time so that there is always a change in the number of players for the groups. So it goes on until only one or two are left as the winners.

Molecules can also be played to music. Then the players have to dance to the music until it stops, and then the number is called.

Aminata stays a while to watch how the others are playing. Then she walks down the hill towards home with Habib on her back.

'It is difficult for girls in Mali to play,' the leader of the centre tells me. 'Girls get all kinds of tasks in the household when they are old enough. Boys can play outside. If any toys are bought in a household, it is usually a ball or a tin car for a boy. Girls have to help with cooking, cleaning and taking care of the little ones.'

He nods at the group that is playing. 'There are quite a few girls in our centre,' he says. 'A lot of parents don't approve of boys and girls playing together. We try to do something about that. With board games and cards it is easy to get boys and girls to join in one game. In the circle games as well we try to mix them as much as possible. One of my favourite games for doing this is Molecules: the kids run in each other's arms laughing. When groups develop where boys and girls embrace, my plan has worked.'

THE FOOTBALL CAPTAIN

A big eagle with outspread wings stands over the green, yellow and red flag of Mali. He is holding a football in his claws.

Mamadou Keita looks at the big wall painting with pride. The eagle with the ball is the symbol of the Malian Football Association *Les Aigles*, the eagles. Mamadou is the technical director of the Malian national team. In the country he is known under the name of 'Capi'.

Capi is short for *Capitaine*, the honorary name that Mamadou has been carrying for years. Capi is a hero in Mali. He was the national coach who made sure Mali got into the semi-finals of the Africa Cup. But not everyone was pleased with Capi.

In a small room of the Association building there are a few league winners' cups; there are pictures of the national team and banners of several national football teams that have played against Mali. Capi walks past all the memories and stands still at a black and white photo. He sees himself sitting there, on the front row, in the national team. Years ago he was a top player.

But football players don't go on forever. Every top player has to decide at a certain moment what he wants to do after his career. Capi decided to become a trainer. He was lucky; he got the opportunity in Germany to get a training course to coaching.

But with Capi everything changed. After he had been working with the players for a while, it happened: Capi's team won the Djoliba / Le Stade match! Capi still remembers every second of the game and his face beams as he remembers the winning goal.

The First Minister was most unhappy about his team losing. What was worse, he was an extremely bad loser! He discovered that Capi was being paid by the Germans, so he put the word around that Capi was a dangerous spy. Capi's life was then at risk, so he had to flee his country.

Capi had to stay abroad for years. But people knew he was a very good trainer – Capi can laugh about it know – so Mali continued to ask for his advice. It took some time, but eventually Capi was once more welcomed as a hero in Mali. Now, as the technical director of the national team, he has one of the most important jobs in Malian football

Once a captain, always a captain!

During the evening before I was to meet Capi, television was showing a Chelsea/Liverpool match. In Bamako, everywhere along the roadside, small TV battery sets were on, outside. In the warm evening breeze everyone would sit close to one another so as not to miss any of the game. All that could be heard outside was the chirping of the crickets and the voice of the TV commentator – except when there was a shot at goal. Then a mighty cheering sound would rise up, always to end in a deep sigh. There was not a single goal during the whole game!
'The whole country loves football,' Capi says. 'Men and women too – we also have a national women's team. When a game is being played, all quarrels and cares are forgotten. Even when the national team fails to play well, people feel for them. The saying, "There are as many coaches as there are spectators," is only too true. But,' he continues, 'there is also a problem, because many boys are so fond of football that they don't go to school. They say goodbye to their parents in the morning around school time and instead of the walk to school, make their way to somewhere they can play football. They all want to go to Europe to become professionals. A lot of children even forge their birth certificates

Afterwards he was appointed coach to one of the most important teams in Mali. Germany paid his salary.

In those days there were two important football teams in Mali who always wanted to win, fair or foul, against the other. These were FC Djoliba and Le Stade Malien. Capi trained one of the teams, whilst the other was owned by the First Minister of Mali.

Before Capi arrived to join his team, they had always lost.

RIGHT TO PLAY

FRUIT SALAD

All players, but one, stand in a ring.
Around the feet of every player in the ring a circle is drawn with a piece of chalk.
Each player gets the name of a fruit. In Quinzambougou all Bambara fruit names are given. So a player is a *namasa*, a banana; a *mangoro*, a mango; or a *limurun*, an orange.
One after the other, all get a name (namasa, mangoro, limurun, namasa, mangoro, etc).
As a reminder of whose fruit is which, the first letter of the fruit is drawn in front of the circle.

The player in the middle does not have his own circle, but has to try to take over one of another player. When he calls the name of a piece of fruit, all players with that name have to change places as quickly as possible. The player in the middle now can try to take over one of the circles so that someone else is left to take a turn in the middle.
When the player in the middle calls 'fruit salad,' all have to change circles.

to pretend they are eighteen – old enough to play abroad – yet in reality they are fourteen or fifteen at most.

I think it is important that sports and education are combined, that children can play sports and can learn, so they can do something other than kick a ball at some future period. Therefore I am proud that Right To Play has asked me to become an athlete ambassador.' As he says this he produces the well-known red ball. 'With Right To Play I can make a difference. I can teach the children something. I can teach them what responsibility is, how they have to cooperate and, equally, how they can lead. And all this in the most pleasantly possible way, through sport. Through football.'

The heat is overwhelming when we get out of the car in Bakaribougou. We have come here to have a look at the construction of a centre made possible by Right To Play. Today it must be at least 113 degrees. The warm sahel wind blows over the red earth like a blow-dryer, covering everything with dust.

It is not just the heat that catches the breath, but it's the stench that hits me right in the face. It smells like rotting fruit and meat, urine and excrement, and fish that has been out for too long in the sun. I'm standing next to an open sewer of which I cannot even see the contents, because the sludge is covered with a thick layer of garbage: car tyres, cans, plastic bags, meal boxes, cardboard boxes, and so on. The streets themselves are also covered in broken glass, food remains, rubber, plastic, metal, etceteras.

A boy comes walking along; he hits a car tyre with a stick like a hoop. Accidentally he hits the tyre the wrong way. His hoop turns the wrong way and plunges into the sewer. The little boy immediately jumps after it. He sinks up to his waist in the black sludge from which an unbearable stench arises. With the tyre under his arm he climbs out of the sewer again.

ROOM FOR EVERYONE

Salif climbs out of the water with his tyre under his arm when his mother comes running along. He manages to escape a swipe from her hand when she wants to slap him, but can't get out of her way fast enough as she grabs him by an arm to drag him behind their hut.

'Are you out of your mind?' yells his mother. 'Do you want to be ill? How often have I told you not to play near the gutters?'

'But my tyre...' Salif defends himself.

'And just now as the guests are arriving,' his mother grumbles on while she empties a can of water over Salif and roughly

brushes him clean. 'That's it,' she says, and she gives the boy a little push in the direction of the cabin. 'Put on your other pants. I'm off now.' She walks away quickly.

Now Salif remembers. There will be visitors who arranged for a centre to be built in Bakaribougou. His mother has been looking forward to it for quite some time, because it was told that one could learn to read and write there. She hopes that it will be the place where she can learn a trade that will bring in some money. 'Imagine,' she had said more than once before now, 'maybe we could even buy food every day!'

Salif can hardly imagine this. Today, as with many other days, there is no food in the dwelling, but he has learned not to think of his empty stomach.

As soon as he has put his pants on, Salif runs after mother. The whole neighbourhood has turned out to welcome the guests. The women put on their most beautiful dresses. The girls have braided their hair ingeniously into complicated patterns, short tails with brightly coloured beads in them or with extensions that make countless fine braids dance on their backs with their every movement. Salif sees that even his friends have put on their best T-shirts. It looks like a party.

In one lengthy procession all walk towards the place where the centre is to be built. Just now there is only a half built fence to

RIGHT TO PLAY

be seen of concrete blocks surrounding the walls of two class-rooms. Yet within four weeks it will all be done.

'Salif!' he hears a call from Kane. 'Salif have you heard it yet?' Kane comes beside him, a little out of breath. 'When all this is finished there will be people coming twice a week to play with us!'

'Is that really true?' asks Salif.

'Come with me,' says Kane as he pulls Salif through the crowd to a man who is standing there with a look of satisfaction at the way the building is coming on. Kane knows that this is Baba, who is always visiting to see how the work is progressing.

'Baba,' says Kane, 'Salif doesn't believe me. There really are people coming here to teach us how to play?'

Baba, laughing, turns round to Salif and tells him, 'Just you wait a couple of weeks! But it really is true; so that you will all be able to come here and play all sorts of games. It's going to be a games centre.'

'But mamma thinks it's being built for her,' says Salif. He feels it's great that he shall soon be able to play here, but his mother has been looking forward to it so much that she is going to be terribly disappointed.

The smile on Baba's face grows wider. 'This is for you all,' he says. 'A play centre for you and a teaching centre for your mother.'

Sari and Kane look at one another. Then they are off and away to pass on the good news to their friends.

The evening closes in on Bakaribougou. As we walk back to the car, accompanied by hundreds of children, I have to watch where I put my feet. Everywhere underfoot there is broken glass and the sharp edges of old tins. As the night falls I am barely able to see where I should be walking, yet all these children have to walk through all this ground of sharp-edged splinters in bare feet or thin slippers. Yet very soon they will have a patch of cleared ground where there will be no fear of whatever lies to trap them, be it sharp to injure or infect them, through all the rotting rubbish where they play. Four walls and a roof seems such a small necessity for making every place just that little better.

THE

Mali is one of the world's poorest countries. Yet what money there is in the country is far from being shared equally. You can see from the list of facts about Mali that the average daily income is € 1.89 per day, yet three quarters of Malians have to do with less than one dollar (€ 0.78) per day.

POVERTY OF MALI

HOW COULD A COUNTRY BE SO POOR?

A thousand years ago all was going well with Mali. It was even one of the richest countries in Africa. That was because Africa's most important trading route cut straight through this land, so of course the inhabitants were able to make a good deal out of it. Yet change was to come as trade gradually took to the seas rather than over land. Mali is landlocked, thus without access to the sea and so its main source of income was suddenly lost.

The country's main problems were to come not so much from human activities but from nature. Mali is in the west of Africa. Two thirds of the land is an area of desert. Barely four percent of the land is suited to agriculture, so unable to yield enough to feed the whole population.

What is more, there are years when not all goes well with agriculture. It seldom rains in Mali, whilst during the dry periods a hot, scorching wind blows across the land. If draught lasts too long, it causes the crops to fail. The desert spreads further and there is not enough water to go round. A mere three percent of Malians have access to safe drinking water. For enough to eat and for the health of the whole country, Mali is wholly dependant upon aid from the outside world.

Solutions are always being sought, but they remain hard to find. There are very few schools in the land, whilst two thirds of the population can neither read nor write. No tourists come to Mali, as there are no beaches for them. Goods are difficult to export or import because the country is landlocked, so there are no seaports. The most important product that Mali has to sell to the world outside is cotton, which does not provide much income.

There is one bright spot on the way ahead: although Mali is blessed with few natural resources, there is gold under the ground. In recent years gold has begun to be mined. This may well mean the coming years could show an improvement in the Malian economy. What matters now is that the profits from the land are properly shared amongst the population.

ISRAEL/

FACTS OFFICIAL NAME Medinat Yisra'el AREA 20,770 km² POPULATION (2005) 6,276,883 CAPITAL Jerusalem CURRENCY new Israeli shekel LANGUAGE Hebrew, Arabic, English RELIGION 80.1% Jewish, 14.6% Muslim, 2.1% Christian, 3.2% other LIFE EXPECTANCY (YEARS) 79 AVERAGE DAILY INCOME € 44,00

FACTS THE GAZA STRIP
OFFICIAL NAME none AREA 360 km²
POPULATION (2005) 1,376,289
CAPITAL none CURRENCY new Israeli shekel LANGUAGE Arabic, Hebrew, English RELIGION 98.7% Muslim, 0.7% Christian, 0.6% Jewish
LIFE EXPECTANCY (YEARS) 72
AVERAGE DAILY INCOME € 1,27

FACTS THE WEST BANK
OFFICIAL NAME none AREA 360 km²
POPULATION (2005) 1,376,289
CAPITAL none CURRENCY new Israeli shekelTAAL Arabic, Hebrew, English RELIGION 75% Muslim, 17% Jewish, 8% Christian and other LIFE EXPECTANCY 73
AVERAGE DAILY INCOME € 1,69

RIGHT TO PLAY

PALESTINE

It is well into the night when our aircraft touches down in Tel Aviv. From the darkened cabin during the approach I have a good view of lights from the city by the Mediterranean. The skyline across the water suggests that of any city of the western world. Yet I am now in the Near East. Four hours ago I was leaving Western Europe under snow and frost, but now, twenty degrees warmer, I can remove my pullover.

I have come to Israel on a visit to the Near East project in Palestinian refugee camps, to see something of Palestine – that land of the Palestinian – and to meet Palestinian coaches and children. Yet, as the Israelis would have it, there is no such entity as Palestine. Look in an atlas and you will find no country officially known as Palestine. It would not do to tell customs that I have come on a visit to Palestinian territories.

There are lengthy queues before the customs desks. The form I have had to complete will tell them that I work in the stage and that I am spending five days in Jerusalem. The young woman behind the desk has to know exactly where my hotel is and the telephone number that will reach me. That being done, I am allowed to proceed. All has gone easier than I had expected.

But a few paces further I am detained again, this time by a man, armed with a machine gun. He wants to know precisely where I have come from, where I am going, what my work is and why I am visiting Israel. I answer him that, in the line of my profession, I do research on how children engage in sport and play all over the world, and that I came to this country to watch the Israeli children at play

With a smile, the man waves me on with a friendly 'Welcome to Israel!'

I heave a sigh of relief. It's a good thing he didn't ask me anything else, for if I had to tell him that I am going to write about Palestine, I was unlikely to be allowed to enter into the country.

I am in.

I have had three hours sleep, and the alarm clock has done its duty. It is seven o'clock in the morning. I am about to be picked up by Erika en Marianne from Right To Play Near East. We are off to Jericho where the refugee camp primary school in Aqabat Jabr has its Play Day.

Breakfast is not quite what I am used to. I am given brown bread with goat cheese, apricot jam and green olives. It tastes sweet, salt and sour at the same time, yet is in fact delicious. The coffee, served in tall slim glasses has its own particular flavour. 'Cardemon,' the man informs me as he fills

ARAB-JEWISH DODGE BALL

A BALL GAME FOR BOTH SIDES

Many games, sports and pastimes appear and re-appear all over the world. Both Israelis and Palestinians confirm that this version of dodge ball is traditional to their respective cultures. Perhaps you know it as well ...

Mark out an area of play and go into it with everyone. There are no teams. Each and every player is for himself or herself.

One of the players throws the ball skywards. After the ball has bounced twice on its return, the game has begun.

The object is to throw 'out' as many players as you can, without getting 'out' yourself.

There are different ways of getting 'out'. A player is out when hit by the ball below the waist. Should the ball leave the play area, the last one to throw it is out. Any one throwing the ball before a bounce is out.

After the ball has bounced it must not be picked up but swiped by flat hand or fist. The ball may not be hit more than once unless touched by a second player.

my glass again. In my haste to be on time, I burn my mouth on the hot sweet drink.

Erika and Marianne turn up in a white jeep from the United Nations. As I get into the jeep and we are about to leave, it feels as if it's part of a film sequence.

Coming out of Jerusalem on the way to Jericho, I notice a car in the other lane being held up by the military.

Marianne follows my glance and gives an explanation. 'That is a flying checkpoint, a mobile border control. As you will soon see, there are checkpoints all over the place between Israel and land still retained by the Palestinians. Everything gets held up at them; cars, cyclists and walkers. It is just as if these were national borders. Passports have to be shown – you've got yours with you, I trust? Have it at hand for we are nearly there. And put away your camera because absolutely no photos of soldiers are permitted.'

We are passing a long queue of stationary cars. 'We may drive on via a slip road,' Erika tells me from behind the wheel. 'Because we are from the United Nations, we have priority along with ambulances and the top people's cars.' The checkpoint looms distantly into sight. First thing I see is a watchtower, a high wooden observation post clad in camouflage materials so as to make it hard to pick out from

the air. Plainly, a blue and white Israeli flag flutters over the tower. Near the top, I can see a uniformed soldier with an automatic weapon at the ready.

Following the sound of an ambulance siren, I can see how the vehicle is enabled to speed as fast it can along the other side of the border post into Israel. To my amazement the ambulance is brought to a stop by armed soldiers who take their time to go through the driver's papers before turning their weapons toward the back end of the ambulance. The doors swing open to reveal the section where the patient is laying.

THROUGH THE CHECKPOINT

Arin hears the wailing of the ambulance's siren above her head.

She lies upon a stretcher under a thin blanket. Beside her is a nursing brother, who takes her temperature. Her mother is here as well. She is holding Arin's hand and is softly articulating texts from the Koran.

Arin had been wakened in the morning by a searing pain to the right of her abdomen. When her mother called her to breakfast she tried to get out of bed, but could not. The pain was severe and she was near fainting when she tried to sit up.

Her mother, slightly cross, came into the room, but taking one look at Arin called at once for her brother to fetch a doctor.

The doctor was quick in arriving and carefully felt Arin's stomach. But however careful he was, Arin shrunk from the pain. 'Appendicitis,' said the doctor to Arin's mother, and called immediately on his mobile telephone for an ambulance.

While mother and the doctor went to the sitting room to talk about what must follow, Arin's little brother came in to Arin and sat by her bed. 'You're going to Jerusalem!' he said, excited. Arin had wanted for so long just once to pay a visit to Israel. Was it all true what she has seen on the television; all those shops full of lovely clothes and a paradise of toys? But she knew that she would never get in to Jerusalem. At the checkpoint the soldiers would send her away at once. Even if she was lucky enough to get in from the other side, it would be by no means certain that she would ever be able to get back.

Now she was really on her way to Jerusalem. Maybe when she was better she would have the chance just to have a stroll through the old city. She shouldn't forget to ask her mother about it.

Arin is shocked from her half-conscious thoughts by the ambulance coming to a sudden stop.

'Checkpoint,' says the nursing brother, 'nothing to worry about.'

The vehicle stays where it is for quite a while. Then the ambulance doors are pulled open. Sunlight pours in.

Before Arin's eyes can close against the strong light she sees the outlines of four armed Israeli soldiers who are going to inspect the vehicle. Arin hears a soldier climb in. She just prays that the vehicle will ride on as quickly as possible. She wants the pain to go; the pain that is now so unbearable that she sees white flashes behind her closed eyes. Her mother is talking with the soldiers about the sort of identity cards they have with them. Arin can feel the way stretcher is tipped over during the search of the ambulance. She bites her lips to prevent herself screaming for the soldiers to go away.

At last she can hear the ambulance doors being closed and they take off again, with sirens wailing, on their way to hospital.

SAMAR'S TALE

Samar is walking through the streets of the Aqabat Jabr refugee camp. She wears a blue and white striped garment over her usual clothing. That is her school uniform.

It is yet early in the morning. She has been up since five so as to be in time to leave the house. Samar lives in Jericho and walks, every morning, the three kilometres to her school in Aqabat Jabr.

Samar's sneakers are soon dusty with the yellow grey desert sand of the Aqabat Jabr street. Samar never ceases to

RIGHT TO PLAY

CATCHERS AND RELEASERS

Eight players are chosen from within the group. Four of them are prison warders; the other four are rescuers. Have the warders and rescuers distinguished one from the other by coloured armbands, headbands or the like. At the start of the game, the warders try to tag as many as they can of the other players, except for rescuers. Any who are tagged must remain stock still until enabled to run away if tagged by a rescuer, and thus freed.

be amazed at the sheer barrenness of the camp. It is something like a village of low white dwellings. Large tanks on the
roofs are placed to collect valuable rainwater, whilst the streets
are littered with building rubble such as chunks of concrete,
general rubble and lengths of steel cable. Texts from the Koran
are painted on the walls, together with the names of those
killed during the war. 'These are the martyrs,' Samar's mother
always remembers. 'They have given their lives for our
Palestine to be freed.'

Straggling along the sides of the streets are growths of yel-
lowing grass, but not a single tree, plant or bush. Jericho,

where Samar lives, is very different. Her town is well named as
'City of the Palms.' Trees are hung with lovely oranges, lemons
and dates. Purple bougainvilleas are in bloom, whilst the scent
of jasmine is wafted through the streets. Yet in Jericho, too,
Samar has seen change. Her mother tells her that it has come
about through the war. Before then, many tourists visited the
town; some to float in the Dead Sea or to take the cable car up
the Mount of Temptation. Nobody comes to Jericho for holi-
days any more. A growing number of shops and restaurants
have closed and have left boarded up doors and windows.

Samar is eight years old, but has never seen a town other

RIGHT TO PLAY

than Jericho or Aqabat Jabr. She would certainly like to, having heard great tales of the city of Ramallah or about Jerusalem, where the Al-Asqa mosque stands at the spot where Mohammed made his ascent into heaven. That is where Samar would really love to go, but her mother has told her that she must get such dreams out of her head. Jericho and Aqabat Jabr are ringed by checkpoints. Samar would never be allowed through.

It is the last street on her way to school, and Samar breaks into a run. She knows she is in good time, but this is an extra festive day at the school. It is Play Day – a day of games laid on by *Right To Play* Near East. For the whole week all junior classes have been busy with the preparations. The six hundred children are divided into five groups, with each group being given its own colour. As Samar has learned, the colours are those of *Right To Play*; and now to do with the games they are to play. Each colour stands for a particular game.

Samar's group is green, the colour representing health. Ibrahim and Rami, Samar's best friends are in the yellow group, the colour for well-being. Other colours include red for memory, blue for peace and black for physical exercise. Samar is satisfied that she knows them all.

She is to start the day with an hour's lesson in one of her favourite subjects, Arabic. In time, Samar wants to be a school teacher. 'That is really just for girls,' Ibrahim had said when she had told him. 'I'm going to be an engineer' he added. 'And me, a lawyer,' calls Rami. Yet no matter how much Samar has been looking forward to the Arabic lesson this morning, she knows it will be hard to pay attention. She just can't wait for the games to start.

'Marhaba, Samar!' says a voice beside her. It is Rami, still panting after running to be in time for school. 'What do you think we'll be playing today?' he asks.

Chatting away they walk on to the school grounds.

We are in the car and approaching the school when I notice a boy and a girl going through the school gate. They walk on in the direction of their classroom.

As we park the car, the high gate behind us is shut at once. The Aqabat Jabr primary school is large; the junior and senior sections together total some sixteen hundred pupils. It is so hot in the afternoons, with summer temperatures rising to 104° F, that lessons are only given in the mornings. Fridays aside, the children attend school every day from half past seven to half past twelve.

The school buildings are long and have two stories in which the classrooms are accommodated. The walls are

whitewashed against the heat, but the balustrades are of a pleasantly light blue. Classroom windows are barred against anyone attempting to steal the valuable teaching materials. I look into one of the classrooms and see the children sitting in neat rows, but at the sight of me the tidy rows scatter as they get to their feet, dash to the windows, waving and call-ing 'marhaba!' (hallo) and 'shu ismek?' (what's your name?).

The Aqabat Jabr children are born and raised in the refugee camp. The majority of them have never been outside the camp. The latest in gym shoes, cool computer games and tempting dishes exist for them only in advertisements. It is at the other side of the checkpoints in the state of Israel, that such luxuries are to be found. In the camp is nothing: not a toy, no sports gear and many children have no adequate footwear. Members of United Nations staff visit daily to dis-tribute thousands of food packets without which many would die of starvation.

Behind the school is another large gate. A man turns open the lock in the metal door to let us through. Before us is a wide play area, a vast expanse of sand divided by chalk lines into sections. Apart from some hoops, a couple of red Right To Play balls, a few bean bags, some orange skittles

RIGHT TO PLAY

and two buckets there is little equipment around the sports field. It doesn't seem much, but is more than enough for endless play.

Beside the field is a concrete stand where spectators can sit. A few are there in full discussion. One is wearing a 'Right To Play' T-shirt. That is Wissam.
Wissam works for Right To Play Near East in Jericho. He is the organiser of today's occasion. Two friends of his have turned up as clowns, whilst another has been brought along to use his DJ skills in taking care of the whole morning's music. Until late into the night Wissam was at it filling paper bags with a few biscuits and a small carton of grape juice, for playing in the sun brings on a thirst!
With their first hour's lesson behind them, the six hundred children taking part today are ready and waiting on the square in front of the school. The five groups are easily recognisable in the Right To Play colours of red, yellow, green, blue and black. The girls are wearing coloured skirts of crepe paper over their striped school uniforms, or else have coloured paper ribbons tied around their arms. The boys have cut out masks in the same colours. There they are, in tidy rows on the school square, waiting for Play Day to begin. As I walk past, they wave their balloons and raise

high the banners they have made for the occasion. A cheer goes up as the clowns approach the square. Happy Arab music is relayed from the loudspeakers as the move begins in a many metres-long conga line towards the playing field. Their hips are swaying and hands are clapping as they sing along to the tunes they know.
Wissam is up on the stand, microphone in hand. The children are laughing at his jokes and at the entertaining antics of the clowns. Wissam, who explains that there are to be five different games and each group will play every game, outlines the rules of play.

The yellow desert sands swirl about as the children scamper from the one game to the other. The sound of music increases, as Play Day gets under way.

DAMS

Wafa' is the gym teacher at the school in Aqabat Jabr. Her country of origin is Egypt, but she is married to a Palestinian and has continued to live with him in a refugee camp. She is the only gymnastics teacher. Should she become ill, there would be no one else to take over her classes. Wafa' is very fond of her work and the pupils are fond of her too. All the juniors meet up with Wafa' twice per week when she gives them forty-five minutes of sport and play. The seniors get one weekly lesson in the gym. 'Sport means so much to my pupils,' Wafa' says, 'because there is nothing for them in the camp. When they are playing their minds are not on armed soldiers, their imprisoned class mates or family members who are dead or in prison, nor on hunger or on thirst; they are simply enjoying themselves.'
Wafa' needs no time to consider which game they enjoy the most; it is Human dams.

Wafa' divides her class into two groups.
The one group has to work out how best to form an impenetrable obstacle course. Then they take up their positions, one behind the other. The first might stand with legs wide apart, whilst the next two kneel and use their arms to form a barrier, then bent over in the form of a vaulting horse, and so it goes on.
The participants from the other group start to move forward, one after the other. The first to go crawls under the legs of the leading 'obstacle', takes a dive over the barrier, vaults over the horse to make a way through the whole course. When he finishes, the next one follows.
When Wafa' has a mixed group (boys and girls from the lower forms still play together) she has boys and girls form separate groups for competitive play. Who will be the first to break through the barrier, the boys or the girls?

Wafa' feels this game is so important because her pupils are always up against barriers in their daily lives. The checkpoints, for example, appear to most Palestinians as impenetrable areas. Thanks to Human dams, the children learn endurance, patience and to continue the search for a way out. The time will come, lively and happily, when they shall succeed in reaching the other side.

Today we have Hani as our driver. He knows the whole area like the back of his hand and he is driving somewhat haphazardly on a short cut to Ramallah. The city has a really nice nickname, 'The Bride of Palestine'. I know the city mostly from television and newspapers. It is often in the news during coverage of the war between Palestine and Israel, when rebellious Palestinians are shown with catapults, Israeli tanks and soldiers firing. Yet as we drive through the city centre, all appears normal; shops with colourful hoardings, street merchants with carts well stocked with oranges and mountains of green almonds, and at the centre of the square the fountain with its well scoured lions is gleaming white. Yet there remains the question as to whether the day will remain quiet. Marianne has told me that an Israeli soldier shot a Palestinian dead in the city yesterday. The tradition here is that when something like this happens, all the shopkeepers close their premises for the day in protest. Yet with so many people brought to death in this city, the shopkeepers find themselves unable to continue closing every time. Every now and then disturbances break out because of businesses remaining open. What follows is a shattering of shop windows as a warning, together with physical harassment of their owners. On the way from Ramallah to Nablus is the Jalazone refugee camp.

On the one side of the road stands the high camp wall, whilst opposite amongst green hills is a Jewish settlement. The refugee camp is in full view of those overlooking white houses.

No outsiders come to Jalazone. Even journalists are seldom seen. The risks are too great; sometimes shots are fired at the camp from within the Jewish settlement. Life is by no means secure for those who walk from Ramallah, such as the school teachers who work in the camp but live in the city.

As I get to know Katy, the head teacher of the Jalazone primary school, she tells me of the dangers abounding on her daily walk to school. All too often she has been obliged to run for her life; yet she continues to return every day.
'I do that,' Katy tells me, 'because it is so important that my pupils can go to school every day. Their lives are so uncertain. The school brings order into their lives. We play with them. Through play they receive pleasure. They learn to work with one another and find mutual trust. Their health improves, and we help them to deal with the occurrences of their daily lives.'
I wonder how it is possible to deal with a war situation just through playing games.

RIGHT TO PLAY

'Right To Play has made up five different modules,' Katy explains, 'each sort of game has its own colour. One of the Right To Play colours is red. Red stands for the memory. To train memory we have the children tell of their recollections. At first they talk about things that amuse them, followed by those that make them afraid. These matters come to the fore during play. 'But,' says Katy, 'the most important thing we do and where the Right To Play games help is that every one in this school comes to know who he or she is. I want my pupils, and their mothers as well, to go and talk with their parents and grandparents to find out where they have come from. I want them to learn their history. Anyone aware of his history is the better enabled to know himself. Whoever has the better self- knowledge has the greater self-confidence. It is with self-confidence that these children will be able to face a better future.

ASSEMBLY

'Salaam aleikum!' Khaled greets the two old men sitting down to their tea on the pavement. They return the greeting, 'Aleikum salaam.' One of them adds the advice, 'Learn all you can again today!'

Khaled is on his way towards the small fenced school area. He is glad that he can go back to school again. It had been a long night and he found it hard to sleep. Since Khaled's father was picked up and detained three months ago, Khaled has lived in fear of any noise from outside.

As soon as Khaled sees his teacher come in he feels a little better. Miss Nada has to come each day from Ramallah. Every midday she makes the promise that she will be back tomorrow. Khaled knows just what can happen.

'Marhaba, Khaled,' says Nada. 'Could you give me a hand to lay out these hoops? We are starting with musical hoops today.'

Khaled is over the moon, for musical hoops is his favourite game. He arranges the hoops on the ground in one great circle.

As soon as all the children are in, Miss Nada switches on the music. As long as the music is playing all run as fast as they can around the ring of hoops. Khaled keeps as close as he can to the hoops because as soon as the music stops, there is a speedy move for all to jump into the nearest hoop.

More than one can share a hoop, but none may have a foot over the edge. Any one unable to stand in a hoop, or arrives too late, is Out!

As more hoops are removed, the game gets more difficult until there is only one hoop left. Khaled stays in the game almost to the end, but he is out at the last-but-one hoop. Then he sits down in the circle amongst the other children. Every morning, Miss Nada asks what they have been up to during the previous afternoon and evening. She asks whom they have been playing with, what they have seen on television and what is being talked about at home.

All have heard of the man being shot in Ramallah. He was Mahmud's uncle, and Mahmud is in tears as he tells them all that his uncle had a knife in his hand, threatening the Israeli soldier who shot him dead. This is discussed for a while, and other children tell of family members that they miss.

After a little silence, Miss Nada asks, 'Who had a nice afternoon yesterday?'

'I did!' calls Khaled, and it is his turn to say something. He tells them that he stayed over for a short time after school yesterday afternoon with Omar. Because Khaled's father is in prison, his mother has to earn their money. What she does is to prepare food in the school kitchen and sell it to other families

RIGHT TO PLAY

in the camp. She is given the run of the kitchen; paying only for the food she makes use of.

Along with the other mothers at the school, Omar's mother makes dolls and coverlets that the teachers take to sell for them in Ramallah. Together, Omar and Khaled have made a colourful drawing that is now pinned up on the school notice board in the corridor. They have drawn a grassy field full of flowers and they portrayed themselves in front of a fine house with the Palestinian flag waving above.

The class now takes a little while to sort out a few plans for the summer camp. Summers last long in the Near East. So as to be sure the children can make the best of their time, teachers in conjunction with the mothers put their minds to making plans for a variety of activities. There is always one fine party ending in a great show in which all the children take part. Omar is keen to play his ud during the closing production. Khaled lets them know that he's going to learn magical conjuring tricks in time for the show and then make all soldiers vanish. The plans are now verging on the extravagant. Laughing, Nada calls the class to order.

'Tomorrow we shall talk some more,' Nada promised. 'But now, really back to work!'

Returning from Ramallah to Jerusalem we are made to stop at the checkpoint. With a broad grin, a soldier takes my passport and the UN passes from Hani and Marianne. He just takes a glance at the United Nations passes and gives them back. 'These cards are not valid,' he tells us. 'You can not cross the boundary. Go back to Palestinian territory.' 'Invalid?' cries Marianne, indignantly. 'Year in year out and every day we come through the checkpoints with these passes. You know that as well as we do.' 'It is up to you,' says the grinning soldier. 'You can go back to Palestinian territory, or leave your car here at the roadside until I get hold of my commanding officer.' 'Just do that,' Marianne tells him.

Hani parks the car, and we wait. A little later there is a rap at my window. Winding down the window, I see three soldiers in front of me, their automatic rifles at the ready. One, who I assume to be the officer in charge, gestures for us again to hand over our papers. A disapproving glance in our direction, and he shakes his head. 'No,' he says. 'not valid. Just go back.' 'Then I shall phone the UN,' says Marianne. 'Get on with it,' replies the officer, 'and I'll ring my headquarters.'

Moments later, both are on their telephones. Marianne on her cell phone is in Arabic, whilst the soldier talks to his instrument in Hebrew. They put their phones down at the same time.

The officer chucks the passes through the window on to my lap and indicates with his automatic, 'Drive on!'

The order doesn't sink in immediately, so we hear a 'Get a move on!' And the officer repeats 'Drive on!' Hani starts the engine and we are off with a scream of tyres into Israel.

One rainy morning I was driven to the eastern area of Jerusalem and to the Israel Tennis Centre, where a twinning project is organised once a week, on Wednesday mornings. Twinning is a coming together, working together and forging a mutual bond. It was in 2002 when the Peres Centre for Peace approached Johann Olav Koss with the concept of having Israeli and Palestinian children playing together. The Peres Centre, founded by Shimon Peres, a former Prime Minister of Israel, is significant enough to get things done through the Israeli government. Right To Play naturally knows all there is about participation in sports and playing games. The two organisations form an ideal combination. Johann agreed without hesitation, and since then Right To Play and the Peres Centre together put forward football

teams made up of equal numbers of Israeli and Palestinian youngsters. They also organise mixed classes at the gymnasium.

As I come in to the tennis centre, there are several groups already on the courts. There are dozens of children to be seen running around together, over the hurdles and through the hoops. Yet however much Arabic as well as Hebrew comes to my ears, I just can't make out which is Palestinian or who is Israeli.

Those who really can tell the difference between the children are the teachers. Naturally they know the children of their own classes. Twinning takes a greater getting used to by the teachers than by the children themselves.

'That Palestinian child won't ever listen to me!' complains an Israeli teacher. 'Plain uncouth, that lot!'

Meanwhile from a Palestinian teacher: 'Look at that Israeli kid laying in to my pupil there! They have no respect for us.'

Yet, as I look around the children I notice that the Palestinian child who pays no attention to the Israeli teacher doesn't listen either to his own Palestinian mistress. I also see the aggressive Israeli youngster giving the treatment to a classmate. The aggravating child will always be there, but in the tennis centre pleasure comes first.

RIGHT TO PLAY

TA' TA' TA'IEH (HA HA HAT)

There is not much needed for playing this Palestinian game. Children mostly use a piece of rag, but could have a piece of paper, a pebble, a piece of plastic or whatever is at hand. Anything does for Ta' ta' Ta'ieh.

All but one of the participants sit in a wide circle. The odd one out is 'It' and takes the object in his hand. As this little song is being sung, he skips round clockwise, tapping each in the circle as they are passed.

This is the song they sing:

Ta' ta' Ta'ieh
Shubakein bi 'lieh
Rin rin ya jaras
Muhammad rakeb ala faras
Wil tubeh weq'et bil bir
Sahebha wahad Faqir
Ghamdo, enekom ya helwin

Which more or less translates as:
Good bye old hat
off our roof so flat
Just skip along loose so far so wide
Mohammed's horse is come to ride
poor man's bag falls down the well
nothing left for him to sell
my very best friends just close your eyes

When the song stops, he or she who is 'It' drops the object behind the nearest in the circle, and then starts to run fast around the circle. The one, who was sitting in front of the fallen object, gets up and tries to tag It before he or she has rounded the circle. If tagged, It must sit out the remainder of the game, within the circle. But if It gets to the empty place and sits down, he or she stays in the game.

It is now the turn of the other player to skip around the circle while the others are singing 'Good bye old hat'.

our turn,' Amir starts to explain. 'And then we had something to drink and we hung around watching Nickelodeon until the bus turned up...' At that instant he knew he had put his foot in it.

'So you're still going, then?' demands his mother, getting really cross. 'You know that your father and I have discussed the matter. It is quite unnecessary for you to play with Palestinian children. They make our lives quite difficult enough as it is. Off to your room! I'm going to phone the school.'

Back in his room, Amir sits on the bed. He can hear his mother on the telephone. Amir tries to hear what she is saying, but finds it hard to follow. The conversation drags on but, at last, he hears the phone being replaced.

His mother comes into his bedroom and sits next to him on the bed.

'Let's hear about it,' she asks in a more friendly tone of voice. 'What have you all been doing?'

Amir begins. He tells her how he with the whole class went by bus to the tennis centre. A bus arrived as well with Palestinian children. How they were divided into groups at the centre. In every group there were Palestinian and Jewish children. That was really strange, Amir tells her, for the Palestinians were speaking Arabic, whilst Amir only knows Hebrew. Yet he had soon made friends with a youngster from the group. His name is Mohammed, and with his fingers he had made it plain that he is six years old – same age as Amir.

'We had made an obstacle course!' says Amir, getting all enthusiastic. 'And we took balls through it, over our heads and through our legs. And next week we are going to the zoo and then I shall see Mohammed again.'

He recoils for an instant, looking at his mother as he realises that he certainly won't be going with the Palestinian children to the zoo. But his mother strokes his head.

'I am going to have a chat with your father,' she tells him. 'Your teacher has invited us to come along and to see how you all play together. You can then show me, which one is Mohammed. Your father won't be too pleased that you didn't pay attention to him, but I think we can get away with it just this once. Playing together doesn't seem to have much harm in it...'

DISOBEDIENT

Amir rings the doorbell of the flat where he resides in Jewish East-Jerusalem. From the television inside he can hear the closing tune of the soap his mother never misses. There is the patter of approaching footsteps. His mother opens the door, but her expression is disapproving.

Crossly, she calls, 'Amir Sjochet! What makes you so late?'

'We had our gym class today and we were the last to have

RIGHT TO PLAY

OVER AND UNDER

COOPERATION WITHOUT A LANGUAGE

One game that children of all ages can play, yet with no need to understand the other's language, is Over and under.
The players are divided into two or more groups of similar size. Each group forms a row, everyone making sure there is ample space between themselves and the ones before them so that a ball can be passed readily in between. The first in the row is given a ball. As the 'start' is called, the first in the row passes the ball back over his head to the one behind. He, in turn, passes back between his legs to the one behind who passes back over and so to continue until the ball reaches the end of the row.
The last to receive it, runs to the front, with ball in hand, and starts the ball on its way again by passing it over head to the next in line, and so on until all the players in the row have had a turn. The first group to complete the round is the winner.

ISRAËL

The conflict between the Israelis and the Palestinians has a long history. It evolves, mainly, over a strip of land between the Jordan river and the Mediterranean. It is a conflict that can be traced back through some three thousand years.

Thousands of years before Christ the Jewish people had become settled in an area of the Near East. They established a kingdom that included Judah in the south and, to the north, Israel. The kingdom's capital was Jerusalem.

The region enjoyed a mere three hundred years of peace but, in the years that followed, the land was regularly invaded by neighbouring nations wanting to occupy the territory. The 'Diaspora' had begun with great numbers of Jews eventually fleeing to every quarter of the globe. During the period of Imperial Rome, at about the beginning of our calendar, most of the Jews were expelled. The Romans renamed the area *Palaestina*.

PALESTINE

There had always been Palestinians, as well as others, living in an area around Jerusalem. However, for the Jewish people now spread all over the world, the land

ISRAELI-PALESTINIAN CONFLICT

remained theirs and theirs alone. The Jews said it was their right because God had promised it to them. It is written in the bible that 'In the same day the Lord made a covenant with Abram, saying. "Unto thy seed I have given this land, from the river of Egypt unto the great river Euphrates." '

From the nineteenth century onwards, Jews began to make their way back to the land that had been Israel, in the hope of creating a new nation of their own. The Palestinians would have none of it. They felt they had been so long in the region that they had every right to stay there. Moreover, they would say, all Arabs including the Palestinians are of the seed of Abraham through his son Ishmael. Thus, according to the bible, Jews may live in the land as Palestinians.

A NEW STATE

Everything was to change from the outbreak of the Second World War in 1939. Within six years some six million Jews had been murdered. To give the Jews their own part of the world to live in, and in an endeavour to make up for what had happened during the war, the United Nations decided that Palestine should be partitioned into two equal parts, half for Jews, half for Palestinians; Jerusalem, the capital city, was to be shared equally between Jew and Arab.

Few Arabs were satisfied with this decision, feeling that if the Europeans were so guilt-ridden about what had taken place during the Second World War, a place for the Jews should be found in Europe. The Jews, however, were glad to have their land returned to them, and decided to rename it Israel.

When the State of Israel was officially proclaimed in 1948, the neighbouring Arab countries invaded. Israel, which already had a far stronger military capability, retaliated and captured more ground than that allocated by the United Nations. During the course of this war hundreds of thousands of Palestinians had to flee the villages and towns where they had lived all their lives.

During the Six Day War of 1967, Israel seized more territory. There are now only two small areas of Palestinian territory; there is a strip on the Mediterranean coast in the south west of Israel known as the Gaza Strip, the other is a piece of land at the east of Israel on the west bank of the Jordan: the West Bank. In total there is a mere four percent of the former Palestine in Palestinian hands.

That is the current situation. Palestinians are perpetrating attacks on Israeli buildings and the people, who feel they have every right to live there. In the meantime the Israelis in the occupied areas show no signs of intending to leave, or returning the areas they are occupying; they are staying put and do not permit the exiled Palestinians to return to the places where they had been living.

A solution to the problem has been anticipated for years. Still, it looks like the situation is slowly changing for the better. In September 2005 all Jewish settlers withdrew from the Gaza Strip. Maybe this is the beginning of the end of an age-long struggle.

THE CAMPS

To provide some help to refugee Palestinians, the United Nations established UNRWA, the *United Nations Relief and Works Agency for Palestine Refugees in the Near East.* UNRWA helps all Palestinian refugees in the Near East. Currently there are over four million. Refugees have found themselves in camps within the Gaza Strip, the West Bank and in the adjoining countries of Lebanon, Jordan and Syria. UNRWA rents plots of land in areas where the refugees can live, and it sees to food, medicine, education and shelter.

Aqabat Jabr near Jericho and Jalazone by Ramallah are UNRWA refugee camps.

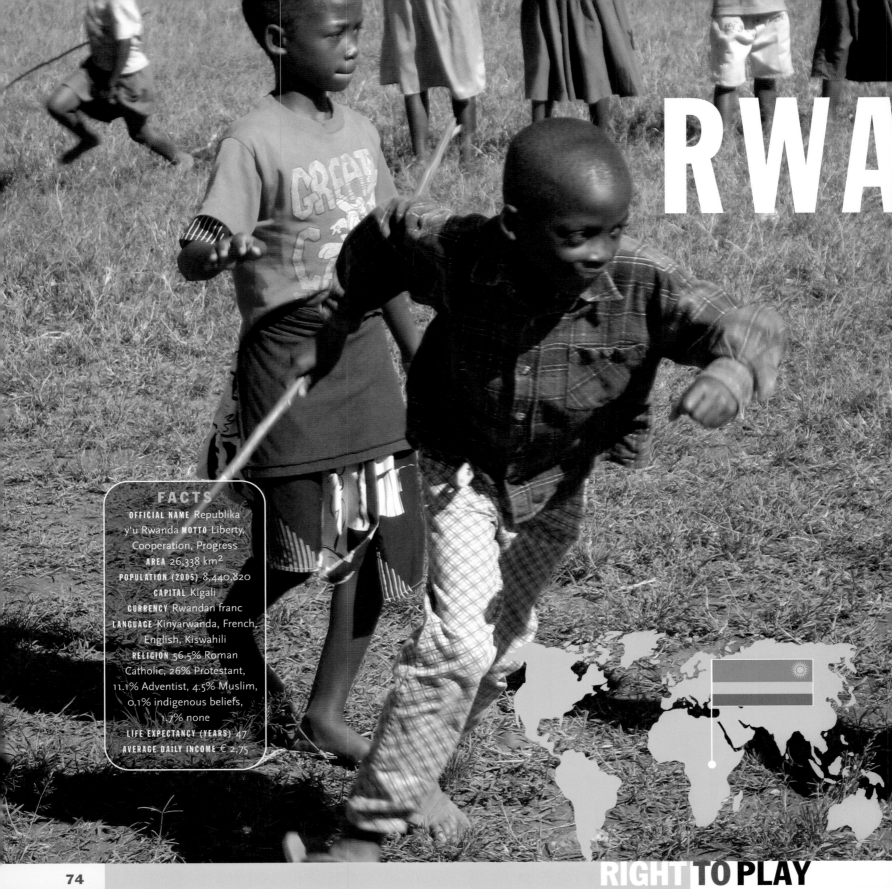

RWA

FACTS

OFFICIAL NAME Republika y'u Rwanda **MOTTO** Liberty, Cooperation, Progress
AREA 26,338 km²
POPULATION (2005) 8,440,820
CAPITAL Kigali
CURRENCY Rwandan franc
LANGUAGE Kinyarwanda, French, English, Kiswahili
RELIGION 56.5% Roman Catholic, 26% Protestant, 11.1% Adventist, 4.5% Muslim, 0.1% indigenous beliefs, 1.7% none
LIFE EXPECTANCY (YEARS) 47
AVERAGE DAILY INCOME € 2,75

RIGHT TO PLAY

NDA

It is six o' clock in the morning and I am about to check in at Amsterdam Airport. This day I'm off to Kigali the capital of Rwanda, in the heart of Africa.

Earlier, at four, I checked for the last time to see if I have brought everything with me: tickets (Amsterdam-Brussels and Brussels-Kigali), passport and, of vital importance, my letter of invitation I will need later on in Kigali to obtain a visa. The letter is from the Olympic runner, Charles Nkazamyampi. He has invited me to come and spend a week visiting playing days and sporting activities at a number of localities in Rwanda, including places with exciting names like Nyamirambo, Butamwa, Kanombe and Kacyiru.

I put my bag on to the moving belt that will take it away to the right aircraft. The person at the check-in, who also operates the belt, takes my passport and tickets, enters something into her computer and looks up at me. 'I'm sorry,' she says, 'but I cannot let you go on this flight, because you have no visa for Rwanda.'

'That's okay,' I explain, 'because I can buy a visa at Kigali Airport. I have already sorted it all out. See, I have all the necessary papers.' I also show her my letter of invitation. She barely gives it a glance. 'An invitation is not a visa,' she says, firmly. 'You will not be able to join this flight.' By way of demonstration, she tears my Brussels-Kigali ticket in half. 'Okay,' I say. 'I still have a ticket to Brussels. I don't need a visa for that. I will get off there and then see how it works out.'

The check-in clerk shrugs her shoulders. She pushes a button and my bag disappears in the general direction of my flight. 'Oh! And yes,' she calls after me as I walk away, 'don't forget to pick up your bag in Belgium, because that too won't be sent on to Rwanda.'

In the small aircraft to Brussels I think about what I will do. My ticket has been torn up. I have no visa. Yet I do have proof that I have paid for my ticket and, of course, Charles Nkazamyampi's letter. I decide to give it a try.

On arrival at the Brussels Airport, I pick up my bag and then walk on to the check-in desks for the Rwanda flight. Standing in line, I look out for the friendliest looking male face, and pretend I have no problems.

At my turn, I put on my most friendly smile. I wish him a cheery 'Good morning,' and tell him I am going to Kigali, but have mislaid my ticket. Showing him my papers, I say, 'Here is proof of payment,' then going on to tell him, 'here is also my invitation to visit Rwanda. There is no visa in my passport yet, but that I can arrange at Kigali Airport.'

As he studies my papers, the man seems somewhat over-whelmed by my story. 'I shall have to check this,' he says before walking across to someone in an impressive uniform. They talk, almost in whisper, occasionally turning to cast a glance in my direction. I encourage them with a radiant smile.

My man returns and presses a button on his computer. 'Alright,' he says, whilst giving me a new ticket. 'I wish you a pleasant flight.'

After almost nine hours of flying I'm standing in front of a counter again. It is warm. Although it is seven o' clock at night, the temperature is in the high seventies.

There is a sign above the counter: 'Visa'. Behind it sits a young man who takes my passport and the invitation. 'Well…' he says after reading the letter. 'If someone wants to send you an invitation, he should ask for our permission first. He just can't do this…' I get a quick glance before he continues. 'But you know what? We'll assume you never got the letter. Here!' He gives it back to me. 'You'll just get a tourist visa.' He fills out a form and stamps my passport.

Relieved, I enter Rwanda.

I am not the only one who has come to Rwanda for Right To Play. Apart from the six volunteers setting up local projects, there are also visitors from the headquarters in Canada, from the American Johns Hopkins University and from the international humanitarian organisation CARE.

Right To Play has set up a programme – Live Safe, Play Safe – in which children learn much, through play, about HIV and AIDS. Before the Rwanda programme gets under way, there will be an investigation about how much children in this country already know about HIV and AIDS. After the programme has been running for a few months, they will be asked the same questions again. It should then be reasona-bly clear if Live Safe, Play Safe has worked and the children have learned something from it.

I'm waiting in front of the hotel, together with the entire team, for the Rwandan researchers who, later on, will question the children in their own language, Kinyarwanda. I take a look through one of the questionnaires: Do the children know people with AIDS? Did their parents die of AIDS? Is it true you can get an HIV-infection from a toilet-seat? Or by getting stung by a mosquito? Or by french kiss-ing? The list runs into several pages.

CHAT ET SOURIS — CAT AND MOUSE

A popular game with Rwandan children is Cat and Mouse.

All but two of the players stand hand in hand to form a large circle.

Of the two players who have not joined the circle, one is the mouse, and the other is the cat. The mouse is in the circle and the 'cat is on the outside. The cat now has to try to catch the mouse.

He might get into the circle by passing under the arms of those forming the circle, but all must try to keep the mouse out of the cat's reach by making sure no gap is made for the cat to crawl through while running round on the outside.

If the cat succeeds in getting in to the circle, the mouse still has a chance. The circle can let him through, but must now try to keep the cat inside.

The mouse can run around within the circle, trying to stay out of the cat's reach. The game is over when the cat catches the mouse.

decent?' She spins in front of Claudette; she has put on her newest dress.

Claudette grins. Her mother is nervous, and that doesn't happen very often. Marie-Jeanne has an appointment with the people from the organisation *Right To Play*. She will be helping with an investigation. There is a Play Day in Butamwa and she is going there to question children on what they know about HIV and AIDS. There are men who will be talking with the boys, whilst Marie-Jeanne and a few other women, will be putting questions to the girls. This is going to be quite something, because girls in Rwanda are not supposed to talk about sex.

Not that this means they know nothing about it. Claudette and her girl friends talk endlessly about what they hear, read in magazines and see on television. But they make sure that no adults can hear them.

In Claudette's class the wildest stories about HIV and AIDS are told. Some of her friends say that you cannot get infected when you make love for the first time, and that you can protect yourself if your boyfriend uses a plastic bag as a condom. Others think the tears or sweat of someone who is HIV-positive can infect you. There is even a girl who claims that AIDS doesn't really exist, simply made up by adults to make sure the young don't have sex. But Claudette knows better. She has been HIV-positive since she was born.

Sometimes, when she looks into the mirror, Claudette sees she's beginning to become a pretty young girl. She can also see it in the eyes of the boys and the men who look at her. Her mother has noticed it as well.

'Claude,' she said the other day, 'you know it won't be long before a boy will be casting an eye on you. Do please be very firm, darling. Be open about it.'

Claudette knows it won't be easy. The men in Rwanda aren't used to girls saying 'no'. Many of them think a woman simply has to do what the man wants. But Claudette also knows it will be difficult to tell someone she is HIV-positive. None of her friends know it, not even Audrey, her best friend. Claudette is afraid she won't be allowed to see her anymore.

Certainly Marie-Jeanne is open about being HIV-positive.

LIVE SAFE, PLAY SAFE

'Claudette, hurry up if you want to come with me,' Marie-Jeanne calls. 'You know I have an appointment! Did you take your Epivir?'

'You don't have to ask that every morning!' Claudette replies irritated. She doesn't like being hurried by her mother in the morning. 'I'm ready.' She takes her notebook and her pencil and walks outside, where Marie-Jeanne is waiting.

'Put your blouse in your skirt,' Marie-Jeanne says after a swiftly searching inspection. Then she asks: 'Do I look fairly

RIGHT TO PLAY

She helps as many people as possible that are also infected. 'People should stop sticking the head in the sand,' she says. 'AIDS is the number one cause of death in Africa. In every second there is one person in the world infected, whilst three out of four times this person is African.' That is why she is so happy with the Live Safe, Play Safe project of *Right To Play*. She thinks it is very important that younger people know how to protect themselves.

At the hotel for her interview, Marie-Jeanne gives Claudette a kiss on the forehead and quickly walks off towards the parking lot. Claudette's eyes follow her. Most of the time she thinks her mother is brave because she dares to be so open, but sometimes she wishes that Marie-Jeanne had never said a thing; that she was like the mothers of the other children in her class, who are not regarded as different.

In the meantime the researchers have arrived. Two mini-buses are waiting, ready to take us to Butamwa. It's not too easy for twenty-one people to fit in amongst the four benches of a small van. I have a window seat and enjoy the sight of terracotta-red coloured earth, the dark green bushes and the brightly coloured flowers blossoming everywhere. I can see tiny bright-blue birds, even smaller than my thumb and butterflies that are bigger than my fist.
Right outside the city centre the asphalted road gives way to a path of tamped red earth through which rainwater has worn deep channels. Yet the driver doesn't slow down; he races through all the ruts at full speed, causing everyone in the car to be thrown around, against the roof, against the sides and against fellow passengers. Slowly, I am turning black and blue.

Rwanda is called the country of the thousand hills and does its name credit. Here and there, the hills of Kigali are so steep that the bus can barely manage. Upward it progresses, at a snail's pace. Meanwhile we all hold our breath, to breathe out again when we reach the top and swish our way down through green ravines.

It has taken almost an hour to reach Butamwa. There are already a few hundred children waiting in the sun. Swiftly they are divided into a few equal groups, and the coaches start the games. While the games are being played, the researchers call the children, one at a time, to go through the questionnaires with them.

As I walk through the streets of Kigali, Rwanda's capital, I become aware that all is very quiet. It is usual in African cities to hear music everywhere. Women sit outside with their wares. Children play on the streets. People are talking, laughing, singing and calling to one another. All who pass by are invited to come and sit down, to have something to drink and to talk. But here it is different. There is no one with wares to offer, no loud music and hardly a sight of children at play. Strangers to the town are regarded as if different. I get the feeling that my strolling along these streets is unwelcome.

Looking on at a game of Cat and Mouse during a Play Day with Pierre, one of the volunteers with Right To Play, I mention what I have been noticing.

'You're right,' Pierre says. 'Kigali is different from other cities in Africa. Since the genocide everyone is suspicious. Sometimes it seems that no one trusts any one else anymore, but that would not be so strange if you could imagine what has happened.'

I can imagine. In a church in Ntarama, a two-hour drive from here, history came to life for me. In 1994 five thousand Tutsi's fled into this church. They locked the door, hoping to be safe from the enraged Hutu's. But the murderers threw hand grenades through the windows, blasting holes in the walls. They went into the church and killed everyone present. They smashed their skulls with their clubs, cut through their heads with machetes or spears, or fired bullets into their bodies. One man survived by pretending to be dead under a pile of corpses. This man showed me around this church where all his relatives and friends had been killed. We had to walk over the pews, because the bones, skulls, shoes, bags and other possessions and remains of the people who died were still there, on the floor.

'Are Tutsis and Hutus playing together now?' I ask, whilst eyeing the children, hand in hand, at the circle.

Pierre makes as if to laugh. 'That is a question you should

RIGHT TO PLAY

TWIPIMISHE SIDA
TI IGABANYA UBUKANA
YARABONETSE

PARTY?

To find out how quickly HIV can spread itself should you do nothing to protect yourself, help is at hand by means of a party. All players get pen and paper. They have to imagine that they are at a party and are meeting people. Each has to ask three other people from the group to write their name on his piece of paper, writing his name on theirs.

When everyone is done, the game leader chooses three players. They stand in front of the group and call the three names that are on their paper. The players whose names have been called are to stand behind the one who named them.

Now the people who joined in call out the names on their list that are written down below the name of the person who called them in line. This way the lines keep getting longer and longer. Is there anyone left?

This is how it works with infection. Imagine that the three players at the beginning of the line are HIV-positive. Imagine too that the names on the paper are the names of people with whom you've had unprotected sex.

By now, everyone in the lines is likely to be infected as well.

never ask in this country,' he says. 'According to the government, no distinction can be made between Tutsis and Hutus. There is only one people, and that is Rwandan.'
'But I can ask you, can't I,' I insist. 'Do they play with each other or don't they?'
'Yes, they play together,' Pierre answers. 'Paul Kagame, the President of Rwanda, is a big football fan. He personally saw to it that football teams were formed in all districts of Rwanda: boys' teams and girls' teams. The government encourages the people to take part in sports together, and by this means, to forget the past. There is not only football but games are organised for volleyball and basketball. It is working, quite clearly. Taking part in sport makes everybody happier. During the game everyone is equal. And you can hear it… On the field there is none of that quiet of the town.'

I'm standing in front of a school on top of a hill just outside Kanombe. It is a long, low building made from yellow bricks. The doors and the barred windows are painted bright blue. In front of the school building, an extensive football field and a basketball pitch are laid out against the slope. Lessons are taking place inside. The classrooms are small and there are windows in two sides. The third wall is one big blackboard, whilst pictures on the back wall include colourful maps of Africa and Rwanda, the physical features of gorillas and cats, together with an anatomical diagram of the human head.
There are three rows of wooden benches in the classroom. The benches are all attached to a table and at each bench, two or three pupils are sitting. Some are diligently writing, whilst others take loving looks at the outside where they will soon be on their way to sports.
When it is at last time for the gym period, all are split into groups that will start, each with their own games of football, basketball and circle games. The pupils play their sports in their school uniforms of light blue blouse and the un-bleached-linen coloured trousers or skirts reaching just over the knee. There are now other children from the locality running up the hill to join in with the groups at play. As the gym period ends, dozens of village children stay on the field with the coaches, and their play continues.

THREAD THE NEEDLE

How's your agility?

All players stand in a circle, hand in hand.

A big loop of rope is tied around the arm of one player. The loop has to be big enough for the biggest player from the circle to be able to crawl through.

Now the purpose is – without letting go of one another – to make the loop go round the circle. You have to sling your arms until the rope is close enough, so you can step through it. Then you sling the rope with your other arm on to the next player.

How fast can the loop go round?

The circle of players can be as big as you like. You can also let several loops – at equal distance – do the rounds and see if each loop is passed on as quickly as the others, or if they end up together.

FOOTBALL FRIENDS

There is a loud banging on the corrugated iron door of the house. 'Jouer, jouer!' Isaac hears a boy's voice calling.

He doesn't speak French very well yet, but he very quickly was to learn that the word 'jouer' suggests 'playing'. This is the sign that games are under way in the Kanombe schoolyard.

Wasting not a moment, Isaac puts on his bright orange basketball T-shirt. He knows the other children think that it is special. A call to his uncle that he's off to play football and, without waiting for an answer, he starts running up the hill to the playground. He just sees that the boy is also knocking on the doors of other huts, or putting his head inside to pass on the news to one and all.

The sun is almost directly above his head as Isaac reaches the terrain. One of the games has already started. He is just too late and there are not yet enough children for two new teams.

He sits down at the side of the field, a little away from the other spectators. Isaac finds it difficult to speak with them. He is from Uganda, a country at the north border of Rwanda. Unlike the people here, they speak neither French nor Kinyarwanda, but English and Luganda.

Isaac has been living with his uncle in Kanombe for a few weeks now. His mother, brother and sister still live in Uganda.

He doesn't think about them too much, because when he does he gets homesick. Least of all he wants to think about that day, two months past.

It was at the end of the afternoon when a man came to their house. Isaac's mother was outside drinking tea with two neighbours. When Isaac heard something break and his mother started to cry, he ran outside. He saw his mother weeping into the arms of one of her friends. At her feet was a broken tea bowl. The other neighbour, cradled within her own arms, was whimpering softly. The man, who Isaac recognised as a friend of his father, walked towards him at the moment he saw him. He sat on his heels in front of Isaac and told him, 'You have to be strong now. Your father is dead. He has been run over by a taxi bus. You're thirteen, aren't you? You are now the oldest man at home. Take good care of your little brother and sister.'

The next days were very busy. Isaac remembers them as if a dream. There were always people around who took care of his mother and brought food and drink. Family of his father

RIGHT TO PLAY

came over and the men held family councils. Isaacs's mother did not have a job and therefore had no money to feed her children or to send them to school. It was decided that one of her brothers-in-law would take care of Isaacs's brother and sister. Isaac would be sent to his uncle in Rwanda once a place in a boarding school could be arranged.

Barely two weeks after the death of his father, Isaac had to pack his things together. He found it hard to keep back the tears when bidding his mother, brother and sister goodbye before getting into the van for Rwanda.

Isaac went to school in Kanombe, but when there were no classes he would stay inside. His uncle felt the boy should go out and play, telling him to 'Go and play football!'

'But,' said Isaac, 'I haven't got a ball.'

'Then sort something out for yourself,' his uncle replied as he turned away, indicating that the conversation was over as far as he was concerned.

The ball problem sorted itself out. A coach often comes up to the playing field, bringing with him a red ball. When he is not around, the boys solve the problem by making do with something they make out of banana leaves, plastic bags and string. Today, though, he can play with a real ball again, and that is far better to play with.

Isaac gets up when he sees a new coach coming with a ball

under his arm. More children are running towards him. A coin is tossed and two boys can choose the members of their teams.

Isaac is proud when he is chosen first. Although they are still having problems speaking with him, his football friends know that he is one of the best players: left-legged and super fast.

The kick-off is soon underway. In no time, Isaac gets the ball. He dashes across the pitch like an orange lightning flash. He strikes, left footed, and... goal!!!

A shaking from a bumpy bus ride, straight up a steep hill, brings us to a plateau in Kacyiru where an enormous playing field is staked out to the size of eight football pitches. On one side against the slope are trees, providing shadow. On the other side, the hill slopes down towards Kigali. There are low houses with colourful walls. I notice children who come running outside to start on the ascent we have just completed.

We are at the Red Cross terrain in which an orphanage for AIDS orphans is situated. These are the children who have lost their parents to AIDS. Many of them also are infected with HIV themselves. Over a thousand children are living here. Three times a week they are gathered here on this field

JEU DE MABIGIBIGI

In a corner of the Kanombe playing field I watch two girls at play. They are clapping their hands, making strange hopping steps and when they stand still they both burst into laughter.

It is a cheery scene, so I ask them what they are doing.

'Jeu de mabigibigi,' one of them says, giggling.

'What does it mean?' I ask.

'Nothing,' the girl says and laughs even louder.

She can't explain to me what they're doing, so I go to their gym teacher.

'Jeu de mabigibigi?' he asks. 'That's something for girls. I can't make head or tail of it!'

When at last I find a female coach who can tell me how it is played, it proves to be really quite simple.

Jeu de mabigibigi is played by two people. You clap in the rhythm of the name of the game: jeu-de-ma-bi-gi-bi-gi, while you jump and hop in time with the rhythm. You decide in advance how often to clap the name of the game and for how long you are jumping before you stop. On the last clap you both stand still at the same time and you stick out one of your feet.

When the feet end up straight in front of each other – so the right foot of the one in front of the left foot of the other – one gets ten points. Ending up crosswise – so both are sticking out the right leg or the left – the other one gets ten points.

You can go on like this until one has a hundred points, or a thousand, or until you don't feel like it anymore.

to play and to take part together in sports. When they are ready and sitting under the trees waiting for their coaches, the children from the dwellings below can see that sports are about to happen. For them it is the starting signal to come to the playing field, for all are welcome.

COACH2COACH

Ziada walks past the trees along the edge of the playing field to find two good sticks. The bamboo sticks she had hung on to from the last Play Day seem to have vanished. Maybe someone had been playing with them and has forgotten to bring them back. No problem, there are enough trees and branches to chose from. When she is satisfied with the sticks she has found, having the same length and of a good strength, she makes her way back to the playing field.

Ziada now knows the names of most of the children that come running towards her. One boy comes close beside her.

'Hey Freddie,' Ziada says to him, 'are you ready for today?'

Freddie, eyes large with excitement, gives a nod. He has not been here for long. At first he was very quiet and didn't want to play with the rest. Then Ziada started talking with him. She told him she knew how he was feeling and how her parents also had died of AIDS. She told him how sad she was and that she still feels sad at times, yet playing together helps

to put a little more fun into life. She had managed to persuade Freddie to join in and now when passing by she always notices he is the first to turn up.

Two years ago Ziada trained with *Right To Play*. She had already been working with children from the orphanage, and had even set up her own foundation, Amahoro, meaning 'peace' in Kinyarwanda. However, when hearing that *Right To Play* was going to give a Coach2Coach training, she knew it was a chance she could not miss. What was so special to her was the fact that she was going to learn how different games give children more than just fun. With the variety of *Right To Play* games she is enabled to make children move, to make them happy and to train their memories. She can give them more self-confidence and teach them how to cooperate or put them on the path to leadership. Additionally, and perhaps the most important to her, she can teach the children many things, for example how it is possible to prevent infection with HIV and explaining the dangers of drugs and alcohol, as well as the importance of taking good care of one's self.

The training was really great; Ziada took part in a variety of games with the other coaches, and even at times began to feel once more like a child. She has now been teaching these games to the children for two years. She can see what she is doing really does work. It is going so well that she creates

new games herself, games that require very few items of sports ware and just need whatever is easily to be found such as a stick or branch, a piece of rope or some pebbles. There is very little sports ware in Africa. Balls, hoops, rackets, clubs, gloves and whatever would cost money; but there is no money. Yet it is not the end of the road, Ziada thinks, and her games are nice enough.

She looks around. Already dozens of children have gathered about her and look at her questioningly. Ziada lifts up the two sticks she found today and calls: 'Who knows what we shall start with today?'

'Estafette!' the children cry out together and they start cheering.

The only piece of sports ware on the Red Cross sports field is a ball. The ball is thrown back and forth in volleyball fashion around a ring, with a coach in the middle. Everyone is mixed in this game: boys and girls, young and old. Young women carry their babies on their hips or in a sling on their backs, so their hands are free to play. From all sides come the sounds of shouted calls and laughter. Clapping- and singing games are played as well. Two groups play estafette with bamboo sticks. Players in a wide ring pass pebbles behind their backs whilst the one in the middle has to guess where they are. Long rows of boys and girls form living

wheelbarrows and race one other. Someone has found a wheel rim. The boys take turns to play with it, and by swiping at it with a stick, they get it rolling like a hoop, down the entire path along the playing field and back. One ball and a thousand children, but no one is bored. Using a little of your imagination, you are always able to play.

A MAYIBOBO IS NEVER ALONE

Denise is over the moon. He walks over towards the playing field where a football match is to be played later on. He is certainly going to watch, but he is not sure about taking part because he has just got some new shoes.

He looks at the ground while he is walking. Rainy season is coming and there have already been a lot of showers that have changed the red earth here and there into puddles of mud. He avoids the puddles with great care. His sneakers are still a brilliant white.

He got hold of them this morning at the mission. He just happened to pass by, something he does regularly to see if there is anything to eat or if some clothes have just come in.

This time he had been really very lucky.

'They are a wee bit big for you,' Magdalene of the mission told him.

But Denise shrugged his shoulders. Such beautiful shoes –

RIGHT TO PLAY

ESTAFETTE

The players are divided into two equal groups that stand opposite to each other at a wide distance in two long rows, side by side. The two groups are facing one another.

In each row the player with the farthest left position takes an estafette stick in his hand. In Rwanda long bamboo sticks are used.

At a signal from the game leader, both the stick holders start running anti-clockwise, behind their own row, over the playing field and behind the other row, until back at the holder's starting point. He hands the stick to the next player in line who immediately starts running the same route. The player who has just returned moves to the back of the line.

The idea during the estafette is to have the runners of one group trying to catch up with the ones of the other group. As soon as a runner touches the other with his stick, his group has won.

YORK

UNITED NATIONS

I'm walking between the skyscrapers, along broad streets filled with cars and with the yellow cabs swishing past. After the red earth of Mali, the dusty landscape of Palestine and the green hills of Rwanda, New York takes some getting used to. I am on my way to the headquarters of the United Nations.

There, a meeting of the Sport for Development and Peace International Working Group is under way. Johann Olav Koss is one of the creators of this working group. He feels that sport and play should not only play a role in the Right To Play projects, but that role should be pursued all over the world, with all governments of all countries. Later on I will be finding myself amongst the world's ministers, athletes and a number of sporting associations, together with United Nations people who will be considering how these aims are to be achieved.

Arriving at the United Nations, I find the first school class of the day is already waiting near the visitors' entrance. Within the hour it will be even more crowded as busloads of tourists swell the waiting ranks to be in time for one of the tours on offer within this building. No less than twenty languages may be employed for these occasions.

THE RIGHT TO PLAY

What a pity the flags aren't out, is what Shaun thinks as he stands in front of the gates of the United Nations headquarters. He has often passed here when no less than one hundred and fifty one flags, from Afghanistan to Zimbabwe, have been flying the length of the six blocks from 42nd to 48th Street. He does however notice the light blue flag of the United Nations: a map of the world, in white, surrounded by the olive branch that is the symbol of peace.

He is on an excursion with his school class from Harlem. Shortly they are to be taken on a tour of the UN building. By way of preparation for the visit, the class has been given some lessons on the history of the United Nations.

The UN was founded after World War II so as to make sure that there would be peace all over the world. The countries that joined the UN did so with the intention of seeing that the world's poor would have better lives, without hunger, disease and war; also to ensure that the rights and liberties of all in the world should be protected. They have been trying to achieve this aim for the past sixty years, but it has not been achieved thus far.

What is especially exciting for Shaun is that he, once through the gates, will be no longer on American soil, but in a so-called International Zone. The teacher has explained that

within the territory of the United Nations, although situated at the East River in New York's Manhattan, the rules and regulations of America no longer apply, as the area is regulated by the rules of the United Nations. Shaun has never before been away from New York, so this tour is by way of a visit to a foreign land!

After passing through the security check, Shaun enters a large hall. There in a corner are neatly suited young men, standing behind a table with nametags. Shaun walks over to it and looks to see if his name is there too. On each card alongside the name there are four logos. He recognises the Year of Sport logo he had seen in school. In the blue colour of the United Nations are printed the letters UNFIP and UNDP, whilst at the right-top corner of the card a red ball is shown with the words 'Right To Play' under it. Shaun wants to have a closer look at this, but his teacher whisks him away from the table.

'That's not for us, Shaun,' she says. 'Stay with the class.'

'What is Right To Play?' Shaun asks.

His teacher looks at him surprised. 'The right to be able to play? You must know what that means?' But before Shaun can explain his question, she gives him a nudge. 'Come along now, the tour is starting.'

While he walks along with the group to a quiet spot where the guide is about to tell them about the history of the United

Nations, Shaun is still thinking about the *Right To Play*. Everyone can play whenever they want to, can't they? After school Shaun often plays basketball with his friends in St. Nicholas Park. There are plenty of parks and open playgrounds in Manhattan, so there is always room to play.

Or would '*Right To Play*' mean that all the children should be able to play on all the playgrounds? There are playgrounds in Manhattan that are only available to rich children. There are those too just for those who are members, but that costs a lot of money. Shaun's sister Jaye is a nanny with a rich family in the Upper East Side. Jaye had told him that in the building where this family lives, there is a special playground where only the children from that building are allowed to play. Yet it is almost always empty when the weather is good, Jaye says, because most children then prefer to go to Central Park.

Or does *Right To Play* want to…

'Shaun,' his teacher calls, 'you're dreaming again!' He sees the class about to walk on with the guide. Now he really must pay attention, or he will be off and away from the United Nations without having seen a thing.

There is a very strict security check before I can enter the headquarters. My bag is searched and I have to walk through a detector gate so the security people can be certain that I am not smuggling in any metal objects. In the hall, my neck is decorated with two name tags that give me the freedom to walk around the building. After some searching, I find my way to the conference room where the first morning meeting is to take place. Tables and chairs are arranged in a semi circle. Before them is a straight row of tables bearing the nameplates of those who will be at the head of the conference.

When everyone has taken their places, I notice that there are two others behind every chair at the table. These are for an assistant as well as an interpreter, for not everyone is fully at home in English – the language in use at the conference. One of the first speakers is Dennis Bright. He is the minister for Youth and Sport in Sierra Leone. He has come to the United Nations to tell the other ministers how important he thinks sport is; not just for children, but also for adults and even for an entire country. He has seen it with his own eyes, yet he knows how difficult it will be to pass on his conviction to all the others. Most people still think sport is just a nice way of spending one's free time, but little more than that. 'There is nothing more stupid than war,' he tells the ministers that have gathered here in this United Nations conference chamber. 'And something as simple as sport can help to rebuild that which has been destroyed by war.'

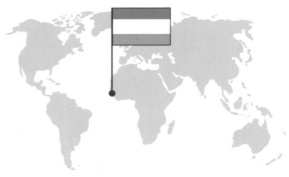

FACTS

OFFICIAL NAME Republic of Sierra Leone **MOTTO** Unity – Freedom – Justice **AREA** 71,740 km² **POPULATION (2005)** 6,017,643 **CAPITAL** Freetown **CURRENCY** Leone **LANGUAGE** English, Mende, Temne and Krio **RELIGION** 60% Muslim, 30% indigenous beliefs, 10% Christian **LIFE EXPECTANCY (YEARS)** 34 **AVERAGE DAILY INCOME** € 1,34

SIERRA LEONE

THERE IS NOTHING MORE STUPID THAN WAR

These are strange times in Sierra Leone. Alhaji can still hardly believe the war is over. He can't even remember what life was like before the civil war. He was four years old when it started; all of eleven years ago.

Walking through Freetown he passes the traces the war has left behind. He is no longer surprised to see the burnt and broken houses, the begging men without hand or arm. He knows how lucky he had been when the rebels invaded Freetown; when thousands of people were killed and two thousand children were kidnapped in order to become child soldiers. Chastain, one of Alhaji's friends, was taken away during the rebel time. Nobody thought he would ever come back, but he managed to escape. Two years on and there he was, all of a sudden and out of the blue, standing once again in front of Alhaji. He told Alhaji how he had lived with the rebels, that he had learned to shoot and had to invade villages to kill people and cut off the hands of boys and men. That time is over now. Alhaji's uncle is sure Alhaji will be able to go to school soon. But Alhaji, himself, is not quite so sure; he wants to see first what the coming months will bring.

Today is a day of some excitement. In Freetown, forty ground commanders are coming together to discuss the future. They are the heads and other senior officers of three different armies that were out for each other's blood during the war. Alhaji can't imagine that it will work out, so when he heard a football match was to be organised to take place before the meeting, and that these chief officers are to be playing, he wants to see the truth of it with his own eyes!

Alhaji soon sees that he is not the only one who is curious about this match. It seems as if the whole town is turning out to watch the commanders play.

As the two sides arrive on the pitch, they are greeted with an enormous cheering. Each team contains men from all three armies and for this occasion the two sides are playing under the names 'Forgiveness' and 'Repentance'. The game is really exciting. When it ends in a draw after ninety minutes, everyone is satisfied. A better outcome could not be imagined.

On the pitch the players throw their arms around one another in warm embrace. Alhaji cannot believe his eyes. Whilst the match was being played, he had totally forgotten these men would have killed each other without hesitation only a few

RIGHT TO PLAY

weeks ago. Because of this game, all argument has been put to rest for a full hour and a half.

When Alhaji walks back home, the whole town is in a festive mood. The war is really over. He finds himself laughing out loud.

'Sport helps!' Dennis Bright tells the ministers. 'Children grow healthier because of it, sport clubs help with the spreading of information about HIV and AIDS and everyone becomes more happy and more cheerful.' Involuntarily he speaks louder. 'Look around you! Then you will see the magical effect that sport and play has on young people – they love learning whatever is on offer during their play. It is high time that governments all around the world understand that their people will simply find improvement through its influence!'

An enthusiastic applause fills the room. Satisfied, Dennis Bright leans back in his chair. His message has got through. Between all the men in dark suits, there is one striking young man. He is sitting in the conference benches in a batakari, a colourful traditional garment from Ghana. His name is Emmanuel Yeboah. He is an athlete ambassador of Right To Play.

FACTS

OFFICIAL NAME Republic of Ghana
MOTTO Freedom and Justice
AREA 239,460 km^2
POPULATION (2005) 21,029,853
CAPITAL Accra **CURRENCY** Cedi
LANGUAGE English, African languages (indigenous groups such as Akan, Moshi-Dagomba, Ewe and Ga) **RELIGION** 63% Christian, 16% Muslim, 21% indigenous beliefs
LIFE EXPECTANCY (YEARS) 56
AVERAGE DAILY INCOME € 5,14

GHANA

RIDING A BICYCLE, WITH ONE LEG

Holding the torch up high, Emmanuel knows he will never forget this moment. There he is, Emmanuel Ofosu Yeboah from Ghana, with the Olympic Flame in his hands. This goes beyond his wildest dreams – and there has certainly been no lack of dreams in his life until now.

It is a miracle Emmanuel is still alive. He was, after all, born with a deformed right leg. Now, in Ghana, many believe that disabled children are possessed by evil spirits. That is why many children who are born deformed, are poisoned or abandoned by their parents.

Emmanuel's father, who was all for abandoning the child, left home. The mother would not cast out her son. Although poor, she raised Emmanuel by herself and carried him to school every day. She would always be saying, 'Whatever you want, you can reach your goal. As someone with a handicap you can stand for something in this world.'

When he was thirteen, Emmanuel went to the Ghanaian capital. What he saw there scared him. He had heard that the handicapped had a hard life, but over there in the streets of Accra he saw what this really meant: that the two million Ghanaians handicapped from birth were being treated like dirt

by those around them. They were being forced to beg for their very existence.

Never, decided Emanuel, never would he beg. He started out as a shoe polisher, but the thought as to how he could change his life and improve the lot of his fellow sufferers would never leave his mind. If only the Ghanaian folk would just understand that the infirm are deserving of as much respect as those without disabilities.

Most of all Emmanuel wanted to take part in sports. Joining in a game with his friends was out of the question; he was unable to participate in the team sport of football. So what was there for him to do? Then came the day when he had an idea: to ride a bicycle he needed no one beside him. He was going to make a journey through Ghana on a bicycle adapted to a one-legged rider; a journey of 610 kilometres. Should he succeed, he would be enabled to make people more aware of the fate of the handicapped in Ghana; but he would do it in the way he felt best, at sport. How surprised everybody would be!

Emmanuel had no money and he had no bicycle, but such handicaps were not to stop him. He wrote letters to companies and foundations in which he laid out his plan. He hoped that

someone would help him. It worked: a Californian organisation built a bicycle especially for him. Before he started out on the journey, Emmanuel got to work writing another miscellany of letters. There were letters to politicians, to ministers, to newspapers, magazines and television networks. Never having tried to ride a bicycle, he now had to learn. When that was done, he was on his way.

Emmanuel's tour was a great success. His story appeared everywhere, not just in Ghana but far beyond its borders there were those who would realise that the situation of the handicapped had to be improved. It presented the disabled with the courage to change their lives. Emmanuel had shown there was just no need to give up. After those 610 kilometres something had changed in Ghana, and Emmanuel was world famous.

Now, as the carrier of the Olympic Flame, Emmanuel has even greater plans. He has received a number of awards, and he is an ambassador for *Right To Play*. He wants to put his fame to the good use of bringing even more change to Ghana's handicapped. He wants to provide grants for scholarships, to raise teams for football and basketball as well as founding a sports school for the disabled.

Here, with the flame firmly grasped within his hand, Emmanuel knows he will succeed. Even one individual can make a difference, so long as he holds to perseverance.

Before lunch, all are on the way to one particular room. What they find here is a whole wall of wide windows offering a beautiful view of New York. The Chrysler Building rises up above the other skyscrapers, and is the one with the tower that looks like a radiator screen from an automobile of the 1930s.

At the dinner, served by waiters that move so softly between the tables that they seem to be sneaking up on the diners, several more speeches are made. One comes from somebody who has brought along balls from all over the world, balls made from plastic bags, of shredded car tyres, woven reed or banana leaves. He demonstrates how children with next to nothing will always come up with ways of making a ball they can use for play, and continues by telling us how important it is to play and to be creative, even when you are grown up. Then one of the world's most famous economists starts speaking. He has just published a book that is called The End of Poverty. He believes in a world in which it will be possible to live without poverty. 'Imagine,' he says. 'In this year alone three million children will die of malaria, yet proper treatment costs less than one euro.'

When he is finished a young woman with a big head of curly hair raises her hand. 'I'm Jessie Stone,' she says. She is an athlete ambassador of Right To Play. 'I heard you talk about malaria and I would like to invite you to come to Uganda. I run a malaria project there.'

FACTS OFFICIAL NAME Republic of Uganda MOTTO For God and My Country AREA 236,040 km² POPULATION (2005) 27,269,482 CAPITAL Kampala CURRENCY Ugandan shilling LANGUAGE English, Ganda, Luganda and other Niger-Congo tongues, Nilo-Saharan groupings, Swahili and Arabic. RELIGION 33% Roman Catholic, 33% Protestant, 16% Muslim, 18% indigenous beliefs LIFE EXPEC-TANCY (YEARS) 52 AVERAGE DAILY INCOME € 3.35

UGANDA

A JOURNEY BY KAYAK, OF GREAT CONSEQUENCES

Jessie Stone studied to be a doctor, but canoeing remains the breath of her life. Yet one of the most beautiful journeys she ever made almost ended in nightmare.

Together with some friends Jessie was kayaking between the crocodiles and the hippopotamuses on Africa's longest river, the Nile. They were paddling through Uganda when two of them became terribly ill. From the high fever, cold chills, muscular pain and headaches, it soon became clear that they had malaria.

Fortunately Jessie knew what they had to do. They went ashore and in Kyabirwa, a Ugandan village, Jessie nursed her friends. When the sick were sleeping she would take a stroll through the village. There she saw to her amazement that no one was sleeping under a mosquito net. How could that be in a country where malaria is the main cause of death? As a doctor she knew that the sickness would be halved, at least, were all these people to sleep under mosquito netting. She made up her mind to do something about it.

In the United States, Jessie thought about how she should best go about putting her commitment into action.

First of all she needed to find out if the people in Kyabirwa wanted her help. So she returned to the Ugandan village to do some research. With an interpreter, she went from door to door and put the questions, 'Has anyone in your family died of malaria? Would you want to buy a mosquito bed-net? Would you like to know more about malaria?'

The answer to every question from all who were asked was, 'Yes!' Yes, family members have died from malaria. Yes, we want to buy a bed net. Yes, we want to know more about the disease.

Jessie had brought with her some cheap bed nets, and explained to those she met that it is cheaper just the once to buy such a net, rather than having to pay every year for anti-malarial medicines. With the aid of sketches and stories, she did her very best to teach the villagers everything she knew about malaria.

While Jessie was working on her project, she met Johann Olav Koss who invited her to have a look at a *Right To Play* project in Uganda.

In Kampala Jessie visited a high school where a SportHealth project was organised. There she was enabled to see how the children were learning something about diseases,

with the help of games. She joined in and played the whole afternoon with children of all ages. Amongst the games was 'Malaria Dodge-ball' which she thought was truly terrific!

Returning to Kyabirwa, she wasted no time in trying out the new games. She discovered they really worked and gave an immediate lead in to the village children's understanding of the importance of protecting themselves from malaria.

Jessie continues to go back to Kyabirwa. She is now trying to start up a local hospital. She has lost her heart to Africa. She gives talks about malaria, but in between times has much to enjoy outside her work. She is staying close to the Nile, at the most beautiful place in the world for kayaking, and she is meeting people from totally different worlds and different languages. Even without recognising each other's words, they enjoy complete understanding; they play together and have some wonderful times.

Adolf Ogi's aircraft has touched down on time, so he will be able to attend the afternoon meeting. The whole group has now gathered in the ECOSOC room, the room where the Economic and Social Council of the United Nations normally holds its conferences. It is fitting that the ECOSOC has the job, among others, to guard the Rights of Man and, additionally, the Right To Play.

Adolf Ogi is one of the most important individuals in the United Nations. He is the Under-Secretary General and Kofi Annan's Special Advisor on Sport for Development and Peace. One should not forget as well that he has twice been Switzerland's President.

Adolf Ogi is a good friend of Johann Olav Koss. He too is convinced that it is extremely important for Sport and Play to have a world-wide role. He tells all those who are gathered in the ECOSOC-room why sport is so important. 'Take Pakistan and India,' he says. 'These countries have been fighting fiercely for years over the territory of Kashmir, yet come together to play cricket. Or,' Adolf Ogi continues, ' look at Israel and Palestine where, due to Right To Play, Israelis and Palestinians play together – something no one would have thought possible a while ago.'

Adolf Ogi goes on to point out that it is not only in war that sport can become part of the solution. Sport can even do much in giving a new sense of strength to the poor, and is a means of providing knowledge through teaching. Through sport it is even possible to give a boost to a country's economy.

Adolf Ogi has recently returned from Brazil where he had been to look at projects using Sport and Play in improving the condition of children from the slums, as well as its involvement towards improvements in the life of the country's prisoners.

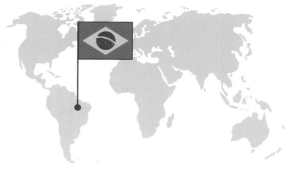

BRAZIL
VITOR'S FOOTBALL

João has been in all morning. He feels as if he is at school. Yet he is a menino de rua. He lives on the streets because his mother's new boyfriend doesn't want him around.
João enjoys the mornings organised by Segundo Tempo. Meaning 'second half', as in a football match.
During these mornings, he and the other street children play games, take part in sports and learn from a variety of subjects.

Each day, straight after his mid day meal, João returns to the streets. He has to make some money, partly for his mother, Maria. He uses the rest to buy something to eat, but sometimes glue. There will be nothing for him to eat at home; there will be no meal for him, Maria's boy friend would see to that. Yet João tries to give his mother some coins every day. He knows she needs them.

To earn some money, João keeps an eye on cars. Today he is lucky because only one man has sent him on his way with, 'Keep away from my car, maloqueir.' However, the next, a homem rico, a rich man with a shining Renault Clio, wants nothing more than João to look after his car. He puts a real into the boy's hand, promising two more if his car is undamaged when he returns.

Six months ago all was different. Then, when João would ask anyone parking a beautiful car if he should look after it, he would wait until the driver had gone before giving his brother the signal to join him. With João keeping a good look out, Vitor would break into the car and try to start the engine as quickly as he could with his self-made tools. If there were anything in the glove compartment, João would get it as a reward. Then Vitor would drive away to bring his new acquisition to an intermediary. No one in the streets of Brasilia could open and start a car as quickly as Vitor, João was sure about that. Yet he was not always quick enough. One night when João at the time was absent, Vitor was caught when he was trying to steal a car. The police found a gun in his pocket, and now Vitor is in prison.

Maria, their mother, tries to visit him every week. She has been told that Vitor has found a job in prison. He makes sports goods such as balls for football, basketball and volleyball. Maria says it is part of a project called 'Pintando a liberdade'.

João says it is a weird name, 'Painting freedom'. What would that have to do with sport? What is most important, however, is that Vitor can earn some money with it, together

RIGHT TO PLAY

FACTS OFFICIAL NAME Republica
Federativa do Brasil MOTTO Order and Progress
(Ordem e Progresso) AREA 8,511,965 km²
POPULATION (2005) 186,112,794 CAPITAL Brasilia
CURRENCY Real LANGUAGE Portuguese, Spanish,
English, French RELIGION 73.6% Roman Catholic,
15.4% Protestant, 1.3% Spiritualist, 0.3%
Bantu/voodoo, 1.8% other, 0.2% unspecified,
none 7.4% LIFE EXPECTANCY (YEARS) 72
AVERAGE DAILY INCOME € 18,29

with the reduction of one day from his sentence for every three days of work. 'And,' Maria says, 'he's learning a profession, so he won't have to go back to stealing cars later on.'

João is starting to get sleepy. The meal he enjoyed at Segundo Tempo gives him a contented feeling and the warm sun makes him drowsy. He hopes it won't be too long before the owner of the Clio comes back. Very soon there will be all manner of activities under way at the playground. There will also be children who live in the favelas, just like him, but who have been to school. João wants to be there. He likes to imagine that Vitor has made the ball they will soon be playing with. This is his way of feeling that they still stay close.

'With the help of Sport and Play I want to create a new generation; a generation for a better world.' Adolf Ogi is coming to the end of his speech, and concludes, 'We are the mountaineers. As a mountaineer you are faced with steep ascents, bad weather and other setbacks. Sometimes you will have a very hard time. You need endurance. But in the end you will reach the top.'

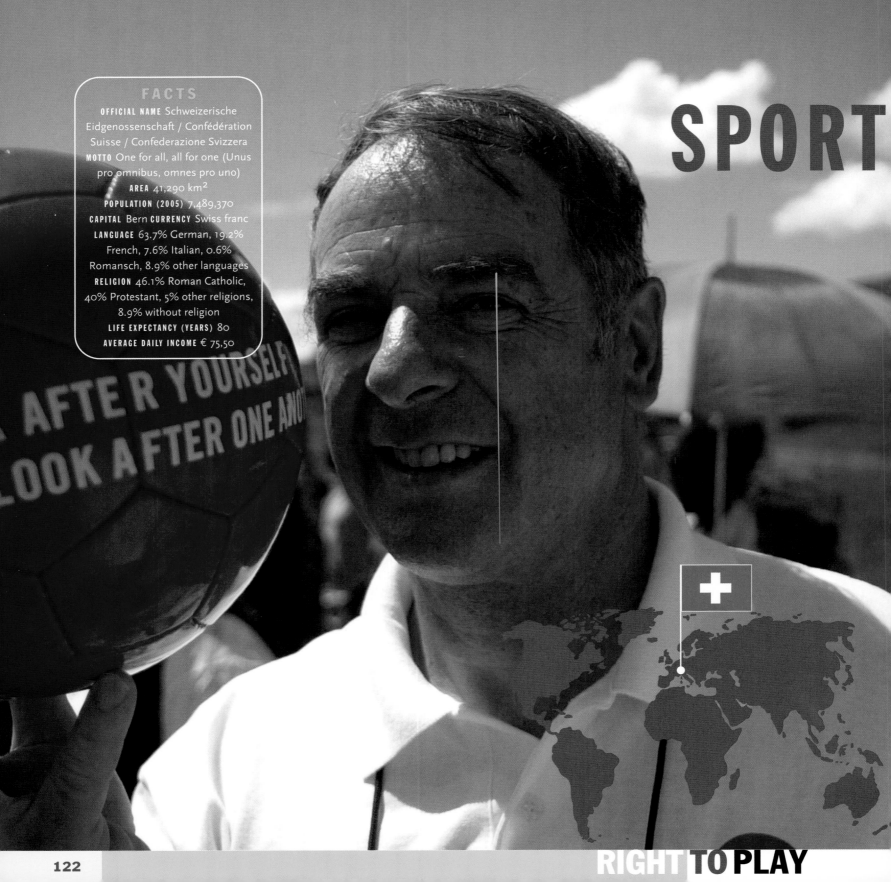

FACTS

OFFICIAL NAME Schweizerische Eidgenossenschaft / Confédération Suisse / Confederazione Svizzera
MOTTO One for all, all for one (Unus pro omnibus, omnes pro uno)
AREA 41,290 km²
POPULATION (2005) 7,489,370
CAPITAL Bern **CURRENCY** Swiss franc
LANGUAGE 63.7% German, 19.2% French, 7.6% Italian, 0.6% Romansch, 8.9% other languages
RELIGION 46.1% Roman Catholic, 40% Protestant, 5% other religions, 8.9% without religion
LIFE EXPECTANCY (YEARS) 80
AVERAGE DAILY INCOME € 75,50

CAN CHANGE THE WORLD

(Former President of Switzerland, Under Secretary General and the United Nations Special Adviser on Sport for Development and Peace)

'I was already taking part in sport when I was two and a half.

I was born in Kandersteg, in Switzerland. My father was head of a local ski-school, so I was very young when I started skiing. I was four when I climbed my first mountain. But it was skiing that remained my favourite sport.

There was a ski slope at Kandersteg's railway station. Every free afternoon we had during the winters, we would take ourselves off for ski jumping. The tourists who were visiting the station would follow our flight from the comfort of a heated carriage. Guests from Britain, France and Belgium would be there to cheer us on the slopes. We would do our best to improve performance at each attempt. If my seven-year old friend achieved a jump of 20 metres, I would do my best to manage 22. There is nothing more satisfactory that that feeling of flight, whether it be through 25 or 30 metres. The time would come when I could fly 40 or even 50 metres.'

'The magic of sport depends in no small measure on the example set by one's parents. If they are not particularly enthusiastic, than you might well turn your back on sport. However, my family gave me no problems in that respect. My father never tired; he would ski, trek through the forests and climb mountains. He made a deep impression upon me, and was the best friend I ever had in my life.

Almost as important as parents are the famous sportsmen and sportswomen, the champions of our times. In the world at present there are some forty at this level who are regarded as heroes, and are an example to us all.

Should a politician be sent off to visit a disaster area, such as to parts of Asia after the tsunami, there are few who would have any idea as to who or what he is. On the other hand, should the likes of Zinedine Zidane, David Beckham or Roger Federer turn up, then there is immediate and all round recognition.

It is of real help to people in disaster areas when sporting champions come to visit them. Playing together, all problems can be forgotten in an instant, whilst hopes of a better future begin to be felt. Maybe someone might be hoping that he will be as good a footballer as Beckham. Yet what is most important is their being offered a belief that they are not forgotten by the outside world and are, thus, no longer on their own.'

'In the year 2000, Kofi Annan, the Secretary General of the United Nations, said "There is the one link that binds the world together, but no one sees how important it is. It is sport. Sport is something that touches the very hearts of the young."

What he said was so absolutely correct. When one travels through Africa, so many come forward with their first question,

"Have you brought us anything to eat?" followed directly by, "Have you brought a ball with you?"

Everyone wants to be able to play. It was Kofi Annan who realised that, and it was the reason he asked me to become his Special Adviser covering all aspects of Sport for Development and Peace.

When I took on this job, I went to New York, to the head-quarters of the United Nations. On arrival I was told that there was one particular individual active in the mission. This was a man named Johann Olav Koss, a Norwegian living in Canada. I knew the name of course, for Johann is famous. He was the Olympic champion with the great thighs who had such enor-mous success in Lillehammer.

It was not long before I met up with Johann, and we found ourselves instantly on the same wavelength. We have since become very close friends. We visited Palestine together. The mayors of all the towns and villages we passed through would tell us of the endless nights when houses were destroyed and people murdered. One said, "All the children here are frighten-ed, all the time. The only way to provide relief for their fear, and to let them forget this despicable situation for twenty minutes, is to have them play together."

I was completely convinced of the veracity of this man's words. I have witnessed it with my own eyes on an occasion when I visited a Play Day in Palestine. There it was that I was able to see the happiness that came to all who were involved; it was simply wonderful. This was an experience that filled my very soul and will ensure that I shall not cease to fight for this project, today and every day. No one has ever been able to change the world, neither the world's political leaders, nor the economists, the scientists, the religious and spiritual leaders – not even the world's media. Yet a better world must be possi-ble; a better world in which all becomes justly divided. A world that will be a better place to live in, without wars and without discord. Sport can make for a better world.'

'To all the world's children I would like to say that sport provides the best way to prepare yourselves for life. You will learn:
To win without becoming arrogant
To lose, yet knowing it is not the end
To respect your opponent
To respect the rules
To pay attention to the referee's decision
To achieve solidarity, integration, fair play and the acceptance of discipline
The better to understand your own conduct
To get to know your own body
Sport is the school of life. That's why it is so important that every boy and every girl should be given every opportunity to participate in sport and play.'

'Sport is valuable, extremely important, and is completely indispensable. It is shameful that there are still politicians who are unable to appreciate these facts; but that is a situation that we, with others, are about to change.

I have always stated that we need some thirty years to ensure a comprehensive change in the world's attitude. We are now planting the seeds, together with Johann Koss. He is fulfilling a prodigious task. He should be recommended for a Nobel Prize.'

THE GAMES IN THIS BOOK

RIGHT TO PLAY

LEGENDA

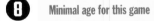 **AL** For all ages

 B Minimal age for this game

 For this game you'll need a flag

For this game you'll need a pen and a card

For this game you'll need a chalk

For this game you'll need sticks

For this game you'll need bracelets

 For this game you'll need a rope

 For this game you'll need a beanbag

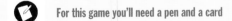 For this game you'll need a ball

Red Mind Ball, *look in the dictionary*

Black Body Ball, *look in the dictionary*

Yellow Spirit Ball, *look in the dictionary*

Green Health Ball, *look in the dictionary*

Blue Peace Ball, *look in the dictionary*

WHAT IS HIV/AIDS?

When precisely AIDS came into being, as well as where and how the disease started, is unknown. The first cases of the disease were discovered in the USA, in 1981. Doctors noticed that a few young men showed the same symptoms, showing a form of skin cancer normally associated with the elderly, or with a rare form of pneumonia.

The doctors who had begun to investigate how it was possible that these young people got so ill, discovered that their immune system – the natural defence system against diseases every human being has in his or her body – was affected. They also discovered that a disease in Africa, slim disease, appeared similar to the new American disease. Sufferers from slim disease had diarrhoea, high fever and rapidly lost weight. Their immune system would not function as it should, so they were often open to infection from tuberculosis, a contagious disease.

THE DIFFERENCE BETWEEN HIV AND AIDS

After two years of research a virus was discovered that has the ability to break down the immune system: HIV (Human Immunodeficiency Virus). Because HIV affects the defence system, an infected individual can become ill very easily. When this happens we call the disease AIDS, which is short for Acquired Immuno Deficiency Syndrome. Because the defence system fails any more to do its task, a person with AIDS can die of a disease from which they would normally recover naturally; influenza or pneumonia, for example.

So, HIV is the virus, the infection. AIDS is the disease caused by the virus. Not everyone with HIV has AIDS. These days the infection can be held well under control with medication. When someone is infected with HIV, he or she is regarded as 'seropositive'.

There are different kinds of HIV. Some types only appear in Africa, others mainly in the USA or Europe. Still new types of the virus are discovered. All types of HIV can eventually cause AIDS.

HOW DO YOU GET HIV /AIDS?

When someone is seropositive, certain bodily fluids are infected with the virus: blood, sperm of the man, vaginal fluid of the
woman and mother's milk. Through these fluids the virus can
enter another body. It can get into the blood through little cuts
or openings in the skin within mouth, vagina, penis or anus.
The virus cannot penetrate skin, so it is only if you already
have a little wound that it can enter your body. It is good also
to know that not all body fluids are contagious: saliva, tears
and sweat can not be the cause of this illness. So you can still
hug, comfort and kiss someone who has AIDS.

HOW DO YOU PREVENT HIV /AIDS?

An infection with HIV can be prevented if you remember in
which way the virus can be caught. You must make sure never
to come into contact with the contagious fluids: blood, sperm,
vaginal fluid and mother's milk.

That is, for example, why it is so important to use a condom when you are having sex: it holds the sperm, so a woman
cannot get infected, and it makes sure the penis of the man
doesn't come into contact with vaginal fluid which could cause
him to become HIV infected.

ABOUT THE AUTHOR

Reading this book, you might have become curious as to who wrote it. Well, that's me, Jesse Goossens.

January 2005 I was assigned to the marvellous task of writing a book about the *Right To Play* organisation. Why me? I think it had mostly to do with luck. They chose me because I had travelled before, because I have been writing books for both children and adults, and because I firmly believe the world can be a better place for everyone.

I met Johann Olav Koss and Frank Overhand, the managing director of the Dutch *Right To Play* office, who told me passionately about *Right To Play*'s works. Their stories were so contagious that I said 'yes' unwaveringly, and set out on journeys to *Right To Play* projects in Africa and the Middle East.

I got to know the countries in a way you can't experience through television or books.

Of course it is totally different to feel the sun actually burn your skin, to be surrounded by music, to smell the odours of other continents and to be able to talk to the people who live there. But apart from that, I went to extraordinary places. I visited refugee camps in Palestinian territories where no tourist ever treads, I walked through the slums of Mali surrounded by lively children, and I danced on a hill in Rwanda at the beat of African drums.

Inevitably I saw horrendous things: hunger, poverty, violence and illnesses. I spoke to children who lost their entire family by means of war, and I met infected children who will never reach the age I am. But what I saw most and for all, was how simple it is to change the lives of these children.

I heard them laughing, saw them playing and noticed how they gained strength and confidence. Each and everyone present got happier during the activities organised by *Right To Play*: both the children, the coaches, and even the people from the neighbourhoods who joined in to watch the children at play.

Everything I saw and heard – in Palestine, in Rwanda, at the United Nations in New York and in Mali – confirmed my believe: Sport and play mean a world of difference.

Right To Play is making life more cheerful for hundreds of thousands of children.

I do hope reading this book has gotten you cheerful as well. If so, start helping, support *Right To Play*, for together we can change the world

Jesse

THE RIGHT TO PLAY
DICTIONARY

Right To Play was founded by Johann Olav Koss, a Norwegian Olympic athlete. The international headquarters are located in Toronto, Canada, and the organisation has offices in The Netherlands, Norway, the United Kingdom, Switzerland, Italy and the USA. In 2005, the year this book was first published, *Right To Play* had projects in Azerbaijan, Benin, Ethiopia, Ghana, Guinea, Israel/Palestine, Kenya, Mali, Mozambique, Rwanda, Sierra Leone, Sudan, Tanzania, Uganda, Zambia, Pakistan, Belize and Thailand. So one might well say that *Right To Play* is truly international!

To avoid confusion, *Right To Play* uses the same (English) names for its projects in every country. All these names can be found in this book. For ease of clarification, they are categorised below.

Words are supported by arrows (→) to indicate that the term may be found elsewhere in the list.

ATHLETE AMBASSADOR

An athlete ambassador is a sporting figure of world renown whose fame is such that it can be put to good use in support of *Right To Play*. The athlete ambassador brings attention to the organisation and explains to communities at large the importance of the aims and intentions of *Right To Play*.

There are athlete ambassadors from North America and from Europe, but also from countries where *Right To Play* initiates projects. That is of special importance, for when young people are addressed by their own sporting heroes, they will be the more inclined to join in the *Right To Play* activities.

COACH2COACH

→ Project coordinators (PCs) from *Right To Play* look for volunteers they can train as coaches within the country in which they work. So they coach coaches. During this training the new coaches are taught a great deal, such as:
- how a child develops;
- how to control a group;
- how to be in charge;
- how problems can be prevented, also how to solve them if they occur;
- how to make a sport and play programme;
- which goals the participant can achieve, and desires to achieve while taking part in sport and play;
- how to deal with arguments;
- how sports equipment and playgrounds can best be used and maintained;
- how to supervise the children;
- how to get people working together;
- what the role of the coach is during sports and play;

- how best to communicate with children and sports clubs, as well as the adults likely to be involved;
- the rules of the various sports and how to observe them;
- establishing and coaching sports teams;
- establishing and maintaining sports clubs;
- → Live Safe, Play Safe;
- → Red Ball Child Play.

Taken all in all, this is quite a programme! However, upon the satisfactory completion of a training course, the volunteer receives a diploma and is thus enabled to start his or her own projects without the help of *Right To Play*. The new coaches, themselves, can now give Coach2Coach training. Should that go well, *Right To Play*'s plan has succeeded, whilst more and more coaches are added without the help of *Right To Play*. When the project is standing firmly upon its own feet, *Right To Play* may leave the country.

COMMUNICATION COORDINATOR (CC)

A communication coordinator works in a → SportHealth programme. As the name of the title suggests, the CCs are occupied with all forms of communication and information concerning the SportHealth programme in the countries they serve. They have to make careful study of local customs concerning sport, games and health care; for every country has its own different traditions, taboos and religious convictions.

The tasks of the communication coordinator include:
- maintaining contact with national and local media;
- making and maintaining contact with any organisations *Right To Play* could usefully work with;
- recruiting → athlete ambassadors and to make full use of them when necessary;
- creating promotional material (flyers, stickers, posters etc.) for a wide variety of purposes;
- producing newsletters, articles and other promotional activities so as to ensure all involved in the projects are kept in the picture;
- organising sports festivals and other SportHealth activities.

In short, a communication coordinator is the face of *Right To Play* in the SportHealth programme. He or she is the person to be approached when anyone is in need of information, or when arrangements have to be made. The CC is also the contact with the head office in Canada.

Additionally, the CC works together with → Project Coordinators at the organisation of the modules →Coach2Coach, →Red Ball Child Play and →Live Safe, Play Safe.

LIVE SAFE, PLAY SAFE (LSPS)

The title of this modules offers its literal meaning.

Live Safe, Play Safe was set up to teach young people the

dangers of HIV/AIDS and what they can do to prevent infection.

The LSPS module directs itself to children age ten and upwards. The purpose is to convey 12 messages through activities and games: everything the children need to know to protect themselves against HIV/AIDS. Six of these messages are by way of being 'life skills'; ways as to how a life can be best lived.

The other six are about knowledge of HIV/AIDS.

LIFE SKILLS

- *Decision-making* – You, yourself are capable of making good decisions.
- *Communicating* – Be clear about what you feel and what you need.
- *Differences between boys and girls* – Girls are the more vulnerable to infection, and that is why they need help to protect themselves; protected especially from unwanted or unsafe sex.
- *A secure life style* – Know your body, know yourself.
- *Self-confidence* – Strong self-confidence is needed in the making of the best decisions, and sticking to them.
- *Discovering your own rules and values* – Your rules and values determine the choices you make. By finding out how your principles and your values are formed, the better choices can be recognised for your selection.

HIV/AIDS

- *What is HIV/AIDS?* – HIV is the virus that causes AIDS: an incurable disease that affects the immune system. Anyone can get HIV and AIDS.
- *HIV infection* – HIV is spread through unprotected sex, by uncontrolled blood transfusions, dirty needles and syringes. Transmission can also occur from an infected mother to her baby during birth or breast feeding.
- *Protection against HIV* – Having safe sex or having no sex at all, by not changing sexual partners too often and by the proper use of condoms, one can limit the risk of catching HIV through sex.
- *Stigma and discrimination* – HIV/AIDS can happen to everyone. People with this disease deserve support and care.
- *STD and HIV* – People who already have a sexually transmitted disease (STD) have a greater risk of catching HIV or transmitting it to others.
- *Look After Yourself. Look After One Another* – only working together, and being honest with one another can prevent the spread of HIV/AIDS.

RIGHT TO PLAY

LOOK AFTER YOURSELF, LOOK AFTER ONE ANOTHER

The motto of *Right To Play* – which is printed on the red ball – reads: 'Look After Yourself. Look After One Another.' In only a few words the goal of the organisation is immediately made clear: a better world because everyone takes care of themselves and, what is more: of one another.

This motto is the only *Right To Play* term that is translated. In French-speaking African countries the red balls bear the motto: 'Prends soin de toi. Prends soin des autres.'

PROJECT COÖRDINATOR (PC)

A PC is a volunteer who does fieldwork for *Right To Play*.

He or she lives for a year in the country where a → SportWorks or → SportHealth programme has been set up. There, the most important task is the organisation of training and workshops in the execution of the *Right To Play* modules: → Coach2Coach, → Red Ball Child Play and → Live Safe, Play Safe.

RED BALL

The red ball is the symbol of *Right To Play*. On the ball the motto is printed: → Look After Yourself. Look After One Another.

The ball makes it clear that the heart of the organisation is shaped by sport and play. The red ball is no mere symbol; it is also for real. At *Right To Play* projects it is played with and used as teaching material. What is more, the red ball accompanies the → athlete ambassadors on their visits, as recognition for *Right To Play* and for actual play.

RED BALL CHILD PLAY (RBCP)

The games in this module are divided into five categories.

Each category is indicated by a different ball-colour.

Each colour represents a separate portion in the development of a child.

RED MIND BALL

The red ball represents the memory, for understanding and intelligence.

Activities with a red ball provide training for the abilities of perception, memory, learning, intelligence, understanding, consciousness and insight.

BLACK BODY BALL

The black ball represents the body.

Activities with a black ball go towards muscular training and strengthening; also for the bones and tendons, heart, lungs and a sharpening of the senses. These games also encourage

the growth of agility and power, together with an increase in reactive powers as well as improvement in coordination.

YELLOW SPIRIT BALL

The yellow ball represents feelings and emotions.

Activities with a yellow ball provide a training to improve awareness and self-confidence; they help in the dealing with sadness and with fear, providing hope, fun, happiness and trust. They make for good feelings of safety, as well as offering the feeling of having control over one's life.

GREEN HEALTH BALL

The green ball represents health.

Through activities with a green ball, much is to be learned about infectious diseases like HIV/AIDS. One learns why good food, physical activity, hygiene, sufficient sleep and a healthy environment are so important. The dangers of tobacco, drugs and alcohol are attended to.

BLUE PEACE BALL

The blue ball represents peace and cooperation.

Activities with a blue ball provide training in working together, thus an ability to play in a team. A youngster may learn how to associate with others of the same age, with family members, with neighbours and with the surrounding of nature.

RIGHT TO PLAY

The *right to play* is embedded in the United Nations Convention on the Rights of the Child. Article 31.1 in the convention reads: 'States Parties recognize the right of the child to rest and leisure, to engage in play and recreational activities appropriate to the age of the child and to participate freely in cultural life and the arts.'

Right To Play, with the assistance of sports and of play, intends to ensure that the world will become a safer and healthier place. Sport truly provides the way to attain this aim; for it brings people together, boys and girls, regardless of skin colour, religion, language, political conviction, descent or handicaps. When people come together and have fun, we have the beginning of a better society.

Right to Play consists of two basic programmes: → SportWorks and → SportHealth.

SPORTHEALTH

SportHealth takes things a step further than → SportWorks.

A *Right To Play* team in a SportHealth programme is comprised of at least two → Project Coordinators and one → Communication Coordinator. They live within the city. They not only work with the local children and adults, but also endeavour to keep in touch with local, national and international organi-

sations; they also provide support of the country's health care. With SportHealth, *Right To Play* aims to achieve three goals. The organisation wants to ensure:

- sports and play being used more frequently as an aid to the healthy development of children;
- every person feels stronger and more secure, together with improved cooperation developing with others, amongst each other and between people and organisations;
- sports and play being used in support of national health care, and in contribution to vaccination campaigns along with the distribution of information about HIV/AIDS and other diseases.

To attain these goals, the organisation has developed several modules covered here for further reading from the listings of: → Coach2Coach, → Red Ball Child Play and → Live Safe, Play Safe.

As there are many areas in which there are few safe and suitable sports fields, *Right To Play* helps by using SportHealth projgrammes for the improvement of existing sports locations, or the creation of new playing facilities for sports and games.

SPORTWORKS

When involved with SportWorks the → Project Coordinators go to refugee camps or areas where, for example, child-soldiers return from war and are in need of rediscovering their place in their community.

Within these circumstances, they set up sport and play projects.

In SportWorks, *Right To Play* aims to achieve two goals: that children can develop on the right lines and to ensure that the community in which they were raised grows in its attach-ment and becomes safer and stronger.

Right To Play firmly believes that the sport and play projects are extremely important to children for three good reasons:

- children are made to feel more secure, both physically and mentally
- their trust in adults is strengthened through the manner in which the coaches interact with them
- with the activities being organised on a basis of regularity, the children obtain a sense of order and of safety

For adults, together with the community the children grow up in, SportWorks is most important because it

- teaches adults the skills needed to organise the children's sport and play projects

INTERNATIONAL
PHYSICAL

- brings adults and children closer to one another
- teaches adults to control their own lives and develop initiatives, so gaining in self-confidence
- gives the adults more faith in a better future, thus leading to a feeling of improvement within the community

To achieve these goals, aimed at adults as well as children, the organisation has developed several modules. These are included for reading, under the following index: → Coach2Coach, → Red Ball Child Play, → Live Safe, Play Safe.

Sport is essential for everyone's well-being. That's why the United Nations General Assembly proclaimed the year 2005 as the International Year of Sport and Physical Education. In November 2003, this was stipulated in a UN-resolution in which sport is recognized as a powerful tool to promote development, education, health care and peace. Under these terms the UN wants to focus on the topic of sport and physical education, in both developed and developing countries. They encourage national governments and sports organisations to pick up on this topic, to give extra support to the sports sector and sport-based programmes and projects in developing countries in this special year, and to raise awareness among the general public.

The UN asks for recognition for sport as a tool to:
- Bring people from socially and culturally different background closer together, thus binding communities.
- Promote economic and social development.

The UN asks (western) countries and international sports federations to:
- Assist developing countries in creating an infrastructure for sports and propagate knowledge about sport and physical education.

RIGHT TO PLAY

YEAR OF SPORT AND EDUCATION

- Develop strategic partnerships with partners in both the sports and the private sector.

UN INTERNATIONAL YEAR OF SPORT AND PHYSICAL EDUCATION – CAMPAIGN

In 2005, the sports programme of NCDO (the National Commission for International Co-operation and Sustainable Development) is campaigning for 'sport and physical education all over the world' in co-operation with all her partner organisations from the Dutch sports and development world.
(www.vnjaarsport.nl)

To inform sports enthusiasts in the Netherlands about the power of sports; to involve individuals, organisations and foundations in sport and development; and to raise awareness about this topic with policy makers, to ensure that more people get access to sports, and that more projects and programmes concerning sport and development are supported.

Right To Play endorses the message of the UN Year of Sport and is partner in this joint campaign. More information about this campaign is to be found at www.vnjaarsport.nl.

NCDO

NCDO (the National Commission for International Co-operation and Sustainable Development) involves people in the Netherlands in international development. Apart from that, NCDO supports individuals and organisations in the Netherlands who devote themselves to improve the living conditions of people in developing countries.

SPORT AND DEVELOPMENT PROGRAMME

By means of the Sport and Development Programme NCDO encourages communication, transfer of knowledge and practical co-operation between national, regional and local sport and development organisations. Since 2001, some thirty sport and development organisations are participating in the Platform *Sport and Development*, gathering twice a year to exchange knowledge and experience. Apart from that NCDO wants to raise awareness with the Dutch general public about development and the role of sport herein.

For more information: www.sportdevelopment.org

AND NOW...

Right To Play's headquarters are based in Toronto, Canada. National offices are to be found in Switzerland, the Netherlands, Norway, the United States of America, the United Kingdom, and in Italy.

At the Canadian headquarters Right To Play engages and trains the international and local volunteers who will work 'in the field'. These volunteers all spend a year in one of the developing countries to implement our programmes with the help of local communities. All communication between the fieldworkers and Right To Play runs through the headquarters. The western country offices of Right To Play have only one purpose: to raise awareness and thus collect as much money as possible to be able to give all the children in the world the possibility to participate in sport and play.

With the money we have collected so far, SportWorks and SportHealth programmes have already been implemented in eighteen countries: in Azerbaijan, Benin, Ethiopia, Ghana, Guinea, Israel, Palestine, Kenya, Mali, Mozambique, Rwanda, Sierra Leone, Sudan, Tanzania, Uganda, Zambia, Pakistan and Thailand.

We try to involve the entire developed world in what we do. Everyone – adults as well as children, companies, municipalities and even government leaders – should join our organisation. To reach that goal we participate in as many sports events as we can manage, and we talk to all the people we meet. We use sports as a means to tell our story, to show how you can change the life of a child for the better, simply by letting him or her participate in sport and play.

We also ask famous athletes to imagine what life is like for a child that can't participate in sport. Sport was extremely important to all these athletes when they were children themselves: some of these sportsmen used to be aggressive little brats, terrorizing their neighbourhoods, smacking anyone who dared to bother them. But through sports they grew up to be well-balanced, self-conscious adults who set an example for the youth. Anybody who realizes how essential the ability to participate in sport and play is for the well-being of children, wants to pass on our message.

And that's what we aim for: we want all the world to know about us.

The people working for *Right To Play* all love sports.

It is fun to exercise, everyone should enjoy it. It is not about who runs the fastest, who jumps the highest or who can climb a rope the quickest – the most important thing is that you feel good and that you have a great time with each other.

If you're one of those children who is always the last person to be selected when playing dodge ball, that's not your fault. Your teacher should take care of you: he should notice in what way you are able to join in and allow you to pick a team every now and then. And your class mates should respect you. Sport is all about respect. That's why our motto is: Look After Yourself, Look After One Another. That's what we want to emphasize as *Right To Play*.

When this book has made you enthusiastic about our projects, you could of course donate your allowance – but that is not necessary. There are lots of things you can do to raise awareness, just take a look at our website: www.righttoplay.com If you follow the link to the kids site, you can see what other children have done for us.

For example, you could hold a talk or write a paper about us. Maybe your school is planning a charity walk and you can support us that way. You might arrange a project week around the topic of *Right To Play* or you can play the games mentioned in this book with your class mates. There are plenty of possibilities.

At the site you can also read stories of the children who are able to participate in sport and play through our activities in Africa, Asia and the Middle-East. You can look at pictures and see the drawings made by these children. And you can upload your own sports stories and drawings.

This way, anyone can contribute to a better world.

Frank Overhand, managing director of *Right To Play*
Netherlands